Messages of the Stars
2003

A book of channeled messages through the original form of astrology

By Jane Elizabeth

Welcome

Hello, and thank you for your purchase of Messages of the Stars 2003.

For the last three years, I have sat down with my spiritual guides and have written out channeled messages through what I know as the original astrology.

Many years ago as I was working on a modern-day astrological chart, I called out to my guides for assistance. I remember telling them that I wanted to be able to read the messages in the stars the way the great prophets of the past did. All of a sudden, my Master Teacher and Guide, Jesus the Christ, visited me. Jesus took the astrological wheel and turned it around placing Sagittarius as the first sign of the astrological house. He told me to refer to this as the astrological house and its twelve rooms. It took me many months and years to finally stop doubting what I had been shown. I went from libraries to bookstores searching for information that would validate this information, and nothing. I spoke with other astrologers telling them what I had been given through my channeling, yet no one seemed to have ever heard of this. I finally reached a point where I just "gave up" and began to totally trust what I had been shown. Every chart I would do, I did by hand, and still do. I have totally accepted this as my truth and have learned to work with this system to create an opening for me to connect with the Highest Spirits That Be.

Messages of the Stars 2003, I feel, is my most powerful book yet. As I sat with my guides to channel these messages, I found myself lost several times in the visions that were coming through. 2003 is an incredible year, for I have seen it all. Our world is changing rapidly for our consciousness leads the way. I saw so many things that are destined to take place in 2003. Many things I absolutely did not want to see, yet when I asked the question "why," I received the answer, which made it easier for me to accept what I was being shown. You, too, are about to receive a higher understanding of life through the messages within this book. I remember, last year and the year before, many people coming up to me and saying, "I feel you were talking about me when you wrote this." I was. And I am talking about you again. This book is about you, and you were all I could see as I channeled and wrote. I open myself to receive your questions and comments. Until then, much love to you always.

J.E.

The Original Astrological House
and
Its Twelve Rooms

Sagittarius (Nov. 22 - Dec. 21) is the sign that represents the individuality, oneness and independence. You are here to learn to stand on your own two feet and represent uniqueness to the world. Sagittarius represents leadership, command, principal, guide, chief and boss, yet must first find / recognize your own unique individuality.

Capricorn (Dec. 22 - Jan. 19) is the sign that represents money and material possessions. You are here to decorate the world. You are the ability to turn a seed into a beautiful flower. You are the designer of all sorts. Make us beautiful!

Aquarius (Jan. 20 - Feb. 18) is the sign that rules speech, communication and expression. Aquarius is the talent. You are the Messenger of the Gods. You are the link between God and the people. You are that which is signified by word or expression. You are here to carry out, relay, convey, disclose, get across, report and transmit. You are our writers, teachers, artists and musicians.

Pisces (Feb. 19 - Mar. 19) is the sign that rules the mother and the home. You are the nuturing one, femininity in authority. You are here to provide the place for God's children to grow.

Aries (Mar. 20 - Apr. 19) is the sign of the child, fun, games and play. Aries is the creative one. You are the recently born, between infancy and youth, forever young. You are here to keep us young, reminding us all to keep it fun.

Taurus (Apr. 20 - May 20) is the sign of health and strength. Taurus is the builder, a person instrumental in the growth of something. You are here to heal the world.

Gemini (May 21 - Jun. 20) is the sign of the Lovers, soul mates, partnership and close relationships. You are the energy of difference, representing and attracting that which is other than the self. You are here to connect us.

Cancer (Jun. 21 - Jul. 22) is the sign the rules sex, debts and assistance. You are here to assist. Cancer is the sign of the giver and one who helps. You are the process of repayment and / or the condition of owing something to another.

Leo (Jul. 23 - Aug. 22) rules higher knowledge, education and travel. You are the educator; the act, process or art of imparting knowledge and skill. You are here to teach the world. You are the law and the government.

Virgo (Aug. 23 - Sept. 22) is the sign of the career / father. Virgo represents our place / standing within the world. You are the person whom one is descended; masculine authority. You are here to direct and show us our place.

Libra (Sept. 23 - Oct.22) rules social and friends. Libra is the gathering of many people. You are here to entertain us, bringing the world together to celebrate the uniquenes of the individuality.

Scorpio (Oct. 23 - Nov. 21) is the sign of karma and spirituality. You are the energy of the past, here to correct the now. To take what is to the next level. You are transformation, you are here to perfect.

Dedication

To my soul mate and partner,
Tim Schweitzer
We had so much karma to clear
and to think,
We're still not done.
Without you, I dont' know where I would be.
Thank you for everything!
I love you.

To my best girlfriend
Cathy Miller.
I love you girl.
Planetary energies promise we will work together.

To my ex-husband,
Otto
Thank you for taking our children and keeping them safe
as I built my career.

And To My wonderful children:
Janelle
Richard
Eric and Erin
I know it wasn't easy being without your mom,
however, I am back,
and I promise to spend the rest of my life making it up to you.
I love you forever, and ever, and ever and ever....

Jane

January 2003

(January 2003)

SAGITTARIUS
NOV. 22 - DEC. 21

Happy New Year, Sagittarius! Last year brought about incredible challenges of the individuality as the Dragon's Tail and Pluto intensely transited your Sun sign, spirit testing you to see just how much of an individual you really are. Well, since you are reading this, I know you made it through. This year looks to be a lot better than last.

This year opens up with plenty of positive energies, lining up in your room of Speech, Communication and Expression. This is your year of the voice. This year, you will finally express your talent / gift to the world through writing, singing, dancing, acting, etc.

I feel I need to tell you to stop living in the past. Sag's have a way of holding on to "what mother used to say." Let it go. The Dragon's Tail will be entering into the sign of Scorpio in April, which places it in your twelfth room of karma and spirituality, assisting you in clearing out all of that old junk that no longer serves you.

Your outer personality (the way others view you) has already gone through an intense cleansing as the Dragon's Tail moved through your first room of Self. Now you must prepare for the tail to perform a cleansing in your room of karma. The past always comes back around. The point of the past returning is for us to get it right. Get what right? Life!

The Dragon's Head has transited your seventh room of partnership and close relationships for approximately the last two years, in the sign of Gemini (ruler of partnership and close relationships), either enhancing already existing relationships or perhaps bringing forth new ones. Many of you fell deeply in love last year with all that went on in your seventh room. Many of you may have decided to part ways, for the challenge of difference was just way too much for you. Either way, I feel that if partnership and close relationships exist within our astrological house (and it does), then by all means, it is meant for this to be a part of our life, whether this is a girl friend, boy friend, husband, wife, mother, father, sister, brother, cousin, niece, nephew, grandparent, whatever. You get the picture. Relationships will continue to be a bit challenging as Saturn continues its transit through the sign of Gemini until June.

(January 2003)

CAPRICORN
DEC. 22 - JAN. 20

Happy New Year, Capricorn! This year starts off very exciting for you.

Planetary energies will be lining up in your area of money and material possessions. This is your time of receiving. The Universe wants to bless you for all the wonderful things you have done for others in the past few years. You have been a very giving soul, and now, all of those wonderful seeds you planted within others are sprouting and bearing fruit. Hold out your hands Capricorn, and allow yourself to receive these wonderful gifts of the land.

Investments will pay off this month, for the New Moon, Neptune and Uranus are all direct at this time, in your second room of receiving. Again, Capricorn, whatever you have invested your time or money into, a re-payment is on its way. And believe me, you deserve every dime.

Planetary energies are also lining up in your twelfth room of karma and spirituality. The Dragon's Tail, Mars, Pluto and Venus will all be tran-siting through the sign of Sagittarius together there. Sagittarius is the sign that represents the individuality. Right now, planetary energies lining up in this area are working to present a vision of your Higher Self to you. That is right Capricorn. You are about to receive a glimpse of your next journey. Many of you are about to attract a situation to you, one you have asked dearly to receive, and now the time comes around for to receive what you have been asking for. However, I must warn you. Saturn will be moving into the sign of Cancer, placing this energy into your seventh room of partnerships and close relationships in early June of this year. Saturn in the seventh room brings forth undesirable chal-lenges through another, and most of what this other person will be re-flecting is karma. I know many of you planted very good seeds in others, and yes, the fruit of that labor will come back around. However, there were other seeds that were planted, and perhaps you didn't even realize it, yet, the fruits of those will return also. I know you will be able to gracefully move through this time. Just remember to pray and meditate when things begin to feel rough. Our spiritual guides are but a whisper away.

(January 2003)

AQUARIUS
JAN. 21 - FEB. 18

Happy New Year Aquarius. Wow! A really big year is ahead for you. Something you have wanted to do for a very long time is about to open up for you in the area of career. Get ready for the Dragon's tail to enter into your tenth room of career and absolutely change everything about who you are within this world. Your place is with the people, Aquarius, and when the Dragon's tail enters into your room of career a new place within this world will open for you. The Dragon's tail will sweep through your area of career (your place within the world) from April 13th, 2003 until December 26, 2004. However, now is the time for you to prepare for this planetary transaction.

An incredible new you have been emerging for the last few years, as Neptune and Uranus have been moving through your sun sign, awakening your spirit and preparing you for the world. Uranus has picked you up and turned you upside down and inside out, totally shaking loose everything about your physical outer appearance. Neptune is bringing forth your spirit through your physical layer. You are from another place, and this year you will express to the world what place that is.

Your spiritual awareness is about to take a huge leap as Mercury goes retrograde and then direct in your twelfth room of spirituality. Be careful of headaches. Mercury retrograde directly above your head will cause intense pressure to build. Release this pressure through meditation and quiet times. Surround yourself with peaceful music and friends. Allow your spiritual family to come in and connect with you through this Mercury retrograde and don't forget to breathe.

As your old career goes and a new one comes in, all of a sudden, your financial situation will pick up tremendously. Uranus, planet of sudden activity will be moving into your second room of money and material gain March 10th, creating a huge opening for an incredible amount of material wealth to suddenly come into your life, that is if you are walking in alignment with your true self. This sudden boost in the area of finances has all to do with the change that is occurring in your career. The old way will go and a new way comes in. And with the release of the old way, a significant amount of wealth follows. The Universe has its way of rewarding those who serve the planet.

(January 2003)

PISCES
FEB. 19 - MAR. 19

Happy New Year Pisces! Right now is a time of preparation, for a new life awaits you.

Planetary energies are lining up in your twelfth room of karma and spirituality, in the sign of Aquarius. Aquarius is the sign that rules speech, communication, expression and the talent. God is speaking to you. Your spiritual masters, higher self and all the teachers around you are communicating with you through your thoughts, dreams and visions. You will receive a vision of the self, pertaining to what it is you are to be doing with your life.

Many Pisces people discovered a new talent last year. This year, you will put that 'new' talent to good use.

Planetary energies are also lining up in your room of career, your place in the outer world. The Dragon's Tail, Mars, Pluto and Venus will all line up in the sign of Sagittarius together this month. Sagittarius is the sign that rules the individuality, representing that you are about to discover your true individuality through the incredible alignment of planetary energies taking place there.

Mercury will go retrograde this month in your room of friends and social, letting us know that a friend may need a helping hand this month. What you do with this situation is totally up to you. Just know we do reap what we sow.

Saturn is preparing to move out of your area of the home, and into your room of the children in June of this year. For those of you who do have children in your life at this time, get ready for intense karma to take place here. Saturn is the Lord of Karma, and is indicating that through the children, you will receive a reflection of the self, whether this is from this lifetime or another. Yet, the most important lesson Saturn will be bringing to you is change. The way children have been parented will change dramatically. Pisces, you are the sign that represents the mother, the nurturing one. The mothers of this world are about to be shown and incredibly intense lesson through the souls who dwell within the bodies of our children. Our ways of parenting are about to go under construction. Good luck Pisces!

(January 2003)

ARIES
MAR. 20 - APR. 19

Happy New Year Aries!

Planetary energies are lining up all around career, travel and meeting new people. Wow! This year open up in a fantastic way for you.

First of all, it is through your talent. What is it you do? Whatever it may be, it is all of a sudden about to take off in a very good way.

The New Moon, Neptune and Uranus will all line up in the sign of Aquarius, placing this energy in your room of friends and social. Aquarius is the sign that rules speech, communication, expression and the talent. For the last few years, Saturn (planet of tough lessons, perfection and karma) has been moving through your area of communication, testing every word you say, and everything you do. As the Dragon's Head and Saturn both moved through your room of communication, a new talent exposed itself. Looking at all of the planets lining up in your area of career, social and travel, I would say you have surely done something right.

The Dragon's Tail, Mars, Pluto and Venus are all lining up together in the sign of Sagittarius, in your room of higher knowledge, education and travel. Get ready to learn something very new, and get ready to do a little unexpected traveling due to your career.

In your room of career is the planet Mercury. Even though Mercury will be moving retrograde this month from January 2nd through the 23rd, its energy will still bring forth a great opportunity to you. And to think, this all has to do with how well you prepared you skill.

A time for you to shine presents itself to you. A huge space within our world has just opened up for you. Planetary energies show, you have done something right. You have done something in its absolute Divine, and now you will have a chance to present whatever this is to the world.

Oh yes, I can't forget to talk about money, now can I? Many people will approach you, wanting to discuss some type of financial business deal with you, and it all has to do with COMMUNICATION!

(January 2003)

TAURUS
APR. 20 - MAY 20

Happy New Year Taurus! Last year was all about you and another coming together in some sort of business partnership. Truly, I hope all went well with this connection.

This year brings forth an incredible vibration for you and another to stabilize a plan that emerged last year. You will attract to you an incredible monetary substance, either in the form of money or something that is equally of value. A dream or vision is about to come into fruition. Something you have often dreamed of or thought about doing is about to be given an opportunity for you to do it. A plan is manifested.

Everyone continues to go through the last bits and pieces of relationship issues. Whether we are in a love, business, or friendship relationship, its not over yet. Saturn and the Dragon's Head will both move out of the sign of Gemini (partnership and close relationships). Saturn moves out in June, into the sign of Cancer, and the Dragon's head moves out in April, into the sign of Taurus, your Sun sign. When the Dragon's Head moves into your Sun sign, an enormous personal strength will emerge. You will find yourself feeling alive, vibrant and on top of the world. Just remember to stay in your highest with all that you do, for Saturn moving into Cancer, into your third room of speech, communication and expression, will test absolutely everything you say and do to see if it is perfect or not. Just take your time when communicating your thoughts and make sure that all you say and do are in the absolute "Divine" of order.

This year opens up with discussions about business for you. Remember, someone will come along to financially support an idea you came up with last year. The physical work is about to take place on this project. Just remember to stay honest in all of your dealings.

Jupiter continues to move retrograde through your home until April 4th. Jupiter is the planet of abundance and expansion. Do you want to expand your living quarters, or perhaps purchase a new home? With Jupiter here in this area, you just may find yourself moving into a bigger place, or expanding the one you have. And guess what else? You can afford it. Taking a look at your financial matters, things are looking pretty good.

(January 2003)

GEMINI
MAY 21 - JUN. 20

Happy New Year Gemini! I am sure last year was quite challenging for you with all that moved through your Sun sign. Well now, most of that planetary activity is directly across from you. Saturn, however, continues to move through your Sun sign until June. Yet, most of that 'self-inflicted turmoil' has passed. The Dragon's Head is also moving through your Sun sign at this time, and will be complete and move on into the sign of Taurus, April 13th. Until then, you may find yourself going through your closets and cleaning them out one last time. Well, that's one last time while the Dragon's head is in this particular room.

A partner or perhaps someone close to you stays by your side. Or perhaps, there will be someone new entering into your life. Pluto continues to oppose your Sun sign, placing its energy in your seventh room of partnership. Pluto is perfecting your relationship at this time; assisting you and the person you are with to become a one-of-a-kind. Marriage is very possible this year for you single ones, and a much improved relationship for those of you already in one.

Last year was an incredible time of finances for you, and Spirit shows me that the wealth that came your way is to be used for your 'project' this year. A plan will ignite and come forth from within, as Jupiter, planet of abundance, moves through your third room of communication. You see how Spirit works? First comes the money, then the plan. We are so used to it working the other way. Save your wealth to finance this incredible idea.

Travel activity is very likely at this time. Neptune, Uranus and the New Moon will all be lining up together in your ninth room of Travel and Higher Education. You see, a new plan / idea will come forth this year, and it may even bring forth a few pleasure trips. This is also a time for new knowledge to awaken from within. Perhaps you will want to study astrology, or maybe some other kind of occult studies. Neptune in your ninth room does peak the interest in metaphysical studies.

Spirit reminds you that Saturn's transit through your Sun sign is just about complete. Use this time to complete the little things. Perfect Thyself.

(January 2003)

Happy New Year Cancer!

Planetary energies are lining up heavily around your area of partnership and close relationships. Cancer people are about to receive a unique gift from one who is very close to you. This gift you are about to receive has to do with a great amount of knowledge, which you, one day, will turn into a great deal of wealth for yourself when Jupiter returns direct in April.

Some of you will get involved in a very heavy love relationship, one that will turn your world inside out. The Dragon's Head is not quite finished in the sign of Gemini. And we already know that while the Dragon's Head moved through the sign of Gemini, it brought together many karmic relationships, for Gemini is the sign that rules relationships. Anyway, the Dragon's Head has been transiting through your area of karma, bringing you into alignment with one your soul is destined to be with at this time, a soul mate. Cancer, you are about to find yourself in another part of the world, for this relationship energy you are connecting with involves many changes in your life, one in particular, a long distance move. For some of you, this will be a state of mind.

Many of you are about to release yourselves from the responsibilities of your families, for life awaits you, and many of you haven't felt this way in a very long time. Well, this does look to be a part of souls path. Personally, I will miss many of you, however, you got to do what you got to do.

Your health and physical body look to be in the best shape it has ever been in. I am very happy for you. I know many of you felt as if you were dying last year, and you were. An old side to your self went away, transformed. A new you is about to emerge, and I want to be the first to congratulate you. You have had a lot to deal with in the last few years, and now you are about to receive your reward.

Again, I am very happy for you!

(January 2003)

LEO
JUL. 23 - AUG. 22

Happy New Year Leo! This year opens up with planetary energies lining up directly across from you in your seventh room of partnership and close relationships. Are you looking to start a new relationship, or perhaps enhance the one you are in? Either way, these planetary energies lining up in your seventh room of partnership promise love. The New Moon, Neptune and Uranus will all be lining up in the sign of Aquarius, the sign that rules communication. You and another are about to do a whole lot of talking, and good stuff, may I add.

The Dragon's Head is preparing to move into your tenth room of career, as the Tail prepares to move into your fourth room of home. With the Dragon's Head transiting your tenth room of career, you are about to become extremely busy outside of the home, and finally, your place within this world will be revealed to you. Jupiter, planet of abundance and material prosperity continues its transit through your Sun sign, expanding many things about you. However, with the Dragon's Head transiting your room of career and Jupiter in your first room Self, I would say this is an ultimate time in your life to connect with the Universe and really discover your part in all of this. The last two to three years have not been the best for Leos, yet, this year and the next ones to come look absolutely wonderful. Once again, the Dragon's Head marks a time of finding / discovering your place in this world. Who you are and why you are here will be questions answered in the absolute fullest.

Right now, planetary energies, the Dragon's Tail, Mars, Pluto and Venus, are all lining up in your area of family members. The Dragon's Tail is marking a time of releasing and clearing the last bit of karma between you and your family members. Considering that Venus is here also, she will soften what may want to come out a little more aggressively through the energies of Mars.

This is a time for Leo people to, once and for all, release themselves from the way they may be feeling about their relatives. Face those you are having a difficult time with. Let them know how you feel. Let them know how you felt when they did whatever it was they did. Clear this energy in the highest possible love, so it doesn't have to come back around.

(January 2003)

VIRGO
AUG. 23 - SEPT. 22

Happy New Year Virgo! Planetary energies are lining up in the area of your health and the physical body. Even though everything looks to be physically all right, it does look as if you and another are about to discuss a big move, and it just might make you a little nervous.

Planetary energies (the Dragon's Tail, Mars, Pluto and Venus) are heavily moving through your area of the home this month, suggesting that a clearing is about to take place there. Looks like you and a family member may have shared a few unkind words to one another about money. You know, money comes and money goes. If you have some to spare, then by all means, spare it. Virgo, I know you are not a "cheap" person. However, it does look as if you might be picking a bit. We all have got to do what is best for the self, for if we don't, we're no good for any one else. Well, I tell you. I am sure you know what you're doing, just make sure that whatever decision you make at this time is made in love.

Planetary energies are also suggesting that whatever issue is taking place between you and another might be affecting your health. When this happens, our bodies are letting us know that there is something deep seated, most likely an issue from another lifetime. Clear these old issues that are making you ill. You have every right to live life in the fullest. These planetary energies are taking place in the sign of Aquarius (speech, communication and expression). What is it you need to say? By all means, please say it!

The Dragon's Head is highlighting your area of career, however, retrograde Saturn is there also. The Dragon's Head wants to connect you with one whom you can do much traveling with in the future. However, retrograde Saturn wants you to take care of your present situation, first. If you are going through relationship turmoil at this time, know that there is someone else to come in. The relationship you are in at the moment shows that you and the other had quite a bit of karma to clear. Perhaps, it has all been cleared, and now you're free to move on. What if you don't want to move on? Well now, that's another story. Planetary energies are suggesting that this is a time of clearing for you, whether you want to or not. Things do have a way of coming back around. Yet, when they do, we usually don't want them.

(January 2003)

LIBRA
SEP. 23 - OCT. 22

Happy New Year Libra! In the original astrological system, you are the sign that rules outdoor fun. You are the gatherer of many people, and right now, Jupiter, planet of abundance, is moving retrograde in your ruling room of the astrological house.

Your life is about to switch directions. The Dragon's Head is about to move into your eighth room of sex, debts and other people's money. And just what does this mean, you may be asking? It means, that this is a time where you are about to closely assist another with his / her plans or ideas. You are a genuine promoter. You are the gift of attraction. Someone around you 'needs' your assistance. Are you paying attention? I sure hope so. For if you are, you will not only receive an incredible gratification for assisting another, there is a great material profit in store also. Yet, this all depends on you. Are you willing to assist?

Now, there is no reason for you to be asking about how to increase your monetary situation, for I have just told you. Assist one around you. There is someone close by who desires, needs and may even be requesting your assistance. Pay attention and help out, for there is a great material reward that is destined to come your way if you do what is necessary for you to do.

Planetary energies are lining up quite heavily around the home front. The Dragon's Tail, Mars, Pluto and Venus will all be moving through you area of communication together this month. Mercury is transiting through your home, and the New Moon, Neptune and Uranus are moving through your area of family members.

Let's take a look at Mercury. Mercury will be traveling retrograde this month in the sign of Capricorn, the sign that rules money and material possessions. Are you considering getting rid of some things? Are you a little anxious for money at this time? Not good! If you are in an anxious position for money, then there is somewhere in your life where you are out of alignment. However, you need not worry. A financial opportunity will approach you, I just don't know if you're going to be up to it. Then again, all is in Divine Order. Perhaps your financial situation is the way it is so you'll accept what's about to be offered. We'll see.

(January 2003)

SCORPIO
OCT. 23 - NOV. 21

Happy New Year, Scorpio! Finally, a new year, huh? This year opens up with planetary activity lining up heavily in your second room of money and your home. Are you wanting to move, Scorpio? Well, if so, an ultimate time approaches. Just don't jump the gun and try to move before its time. Even though the feeling is there and it may be strong, make sure that all is clear and hassle free. This is when you know you are working with Divine Order. And just when is the right time? Wait for Mercury to return direct on the 23rd.

For those of you who are walking in alignment with your highest path, there are four incredible planetary aspects transiting your second room of money and material possessions right now. There is the Dragon's Tail sweeping through this area, assisting you in clearing out all that is no longer necessary in your life. The Tail is assisting you in making a place for the higher gifts of the Universe.

Next, we have Mars moving through this area, strengthening your individuality so that, what you do receive at this time, is a direct reflection of your character.

Next there is Pluto. Pluto has been in this area for quite some time and will continue to move through this area until late November 2008. Pluto is the planet of perfection. In order for any Scorpio to receive through this Pluto transit in the second room, one must become as strong and as "God' as Pluto. Walking in your absolute highest will be represented by your material wealth.

And last yet not at all least is Venus. Venus, planet of love, beauty and attraction transits your second room of money and material gain, also enhancing your pocket book. Once again, that is if you are walking in alignment with your highest spiritual path.

Either way Scorpio, this is a great time of receiving for you. Just know that retrograde Saturn is opposing this area at this time, and will go direct February 22nd, possibly taking some of this hard earned income and using it to pay off a debt or two. So you may want to take your time before going on that wild shopping spree.

February 2003

(February 2003)

SAGITTARIUS
NOV. 22 - DEC. 21

Sagittarius, you are the sign who represents oneness, individuality and the "I Am." Your life's purpose is to learn independence, to stand as one on your own two feet. I know there have been many times throughout this lifetime where expressing your individuality has been really tough. Yet, you know what? Once you get through the "toughness," you will be "at one" with yourself, attracting everything you have ever wanted into your life. This time is called "fulfillment."

Many of you are going through a time where a significant talent is emerging from within. Planetary energies are bringing forth a talent. Some of you may have more than one, however, all of you will have at least one. There is an energy and motivation to express the self. A feeling to use the voice a little more than you have been lately. You may be feeling as if there is a great deal to say to the people, and you want to say it all. Spirit advises you to write down these mighty thoughts. Express what you are feeling are want to say to the world on paper, for people may not be willing to hear what you have to say at this time. However, communication is definitely strong for you at this time. Do something constructive with it. You will get your chance to present these thoughts one day. However, for now, use this time to perfect what it is you want to say. Some of you will want to draw and paint. Maybe it's photography. Who knows what your talent is. Who knows how you will choose to express it. Yet, however you choose, by all means, put forth your absolute best, and do all in your highest.

At this particular time in your life, you may be wondering about personal relationships or career, or may even money. Everything and all that is on your mind at this time has to do with the way you carry yourself within the world, has to do with how you choose to express your individuality. Do you desire to express yourself through being a tough person? Perhaps you choose to be simple, or maybe even sexy. How are you choosing to express yourself to others and the world? This has all to do with your personal relationships, money, career, friends, and so on. This is a time for you to bring forth your best and remember what mother used to say when you were growing up. Take what is good for you and use it to make yourself the best person you can be. Remember, you have all to do with what comes to you.

(February 2003)

CAPRICORN
DEC. 22 - JAN. 20

The first message I want to share with you is about your health. Spirit is asking you to pay attention to your physical body especially in the area of the mouth, teeth, gums, lips and so forth. On the spiritual level, when we attract problems with our mouth. it is usually a sign of communication. What are you saying to and about others that is not in the highest? Attracting problems with the mouth, teeth, gums and throat are signs that you are not speaking in your highest. If your teeth are decaying, then "rotten" things are coming out of your mouth. If your throat is sore, you're not saying all that needs to said. If your gums are sore or perhaps you have attracted a fever blister, once again, something pretty awful has been passing through your mouth and your mouth is letting you know. Tell the truth, the whole truth and nothing but the truth, and you will avoid problems with your mouth.

An idea comes in this month, one that is destined to make you a lot of money, that is, if your communication is in the highest.

Planetary energies are blessing you greatly, creating a huge opening for the Universe to bestow its blessings upon you. Venus, Neptune, Mercury and Uranus,, will all line up together in the sign of Aquarius, in your room of money and material receiving. I hope you have walked in your highest and have been the best you can be, for the power of the Universe will now rain down its gifts upon those who have.

And, speaking of Spirit, this is a Divine time for you to connect with yours. Planetary energies moving through your twelfth room at this time are creating a very large opening for you to hear and receive messages from your spirit guides. Take whatever your daily situations and issues are directly to spirit.

This is also a time of karma for you. Things of the past are finding their way back to you. Something you asked to receive is about to be given to you. You know, it all had to do with the power of your words. What is it you are wanting? What is it you desire to receive? Words are power, that is, if you are using them in the highest. Figure out the right words to say in order to attract that which you desire and watch a miracle occur. It's all in your communication.

(February 2003)

AQUARIUS
JAN. 21 - FEB. 18

Aquarius, you will attract an offering of some kind from one whom you may consider a close friend. Pay attention to this proposition, for it will prove to be exactly what you need.

You are magnificent these days. Planetary energies (Venus, Neptune, Mercury and Uranus) are all lining up in your Sun sign, intensifying your outer beauty, making it very easy for you to attract incredible opportunities to you. Work as best you can with what you have. Your outer appearance is about to express itself abundantly.

What is it you want this day, Aquarius? Do you know? Planetary energies moving through your Sun sign at this time says your outer appearance is taking on the form of all you desire to attract to you. And just what does that mean? It means whatever you desire to attract to you, you must know its energy and allow yourself to be like it. Then, you will find that what you want comes right away. Become what you "want."

In the last few years, your social life has changed greatly. This is due to the lesson of the planetary energies that are there. Pluto first moved into this area of your life in January of 1995. The Dragon's Tail moved into this space in October 2001. Both planetary energies are moving through the sign of Sagittarius. Sagittarius represents the individuality, oneness. This time has brought 'one' to you who represents "perfect individuality." This person is a representation of your soul. One day, your soul will come forth and you will find yourself in a position like this one. Planetary energies have dismissed all but one from your life at this time, representing to you, one who stands in their highest. This is where you are headed.

Prepare for the sweeping of the Dragon's Tail to enter into your tenth room of Career / Father in April. Things are about to change. The Dragon's Tail will be entering into the sign of Scorpio (karma), bringing something that you have always wanted to do back around. Planetary energies are also asking you to prepare for the transition of the father, or a father role in your life. One whom you have looked up to as a masculine role model will soon part ways. If there is anything that needs to said or cleared, you may want to do so now. At least you know.

(February 2003)

PISCES
FEB. 19 - MAR. 19

Pisces, you are in preparation for the birth of a new you. Planetary energies are lining up in your twelfth room of karma and spirituality. You are hearing the voice of God. You are receiving visions from above and beyond. Your psyche has enhanced tremendously. Communicate with your Spirit and let it know who you desire to be. Or perhaps, you will want to see who your Spirit is and be one with it. As always, it is your choice.

Spirit says that old stuff from the past is coming up and this is what is affecting your health. Seeds planted a long time ago are coming up and out, back and around. Clear the weeds. If you don't, it will make you ill. Your mind will become chaotic and you will find yourself dealing with severe headaches. Do as less driving as you possibly can at this time. Do your best to keep yourself calm.

Pisces, you are the sign that represents the mother and the home. Planetary energies have been working intensely to get you back in alignment with who you really are. If you are one of those Pisces people who stayed put in your out-of-the-home job, I am sure your physical body is feeling it now. Mars crosses Pluto this month shaking up the energy in your career, presenting a time for change.

The Universe has been working to connect you with your place in this world. Resistance is what will bring you down. For those of you still connected with work outside of your home, release it. Let it go. Tie up loose ends and move on. Use what is left of these planetary transits and move your career into the home. It is time for you to do your own thing.

Planetary energies have been working to improve your home life. For many of you, a serious partnership / close relationship took place last year. You and another came together to enhance your personal lives. Both of you, hopefully, are aligning with your true identity. Saturn returns direct this month, bringing forth its energy of change and perfection. All Saturn really wants to do here is assist you in making your home life as successful as possible. Saturn is transiting through the sign of Gemini (relationships) providing a time of karmic clearing between you and the one you are with. Hang in there. All is good.

(February 2003)

ARIES
MAR. 20 - APR. 19

Life for Aries has been all about communication, expression and realizing your talent for the last two years. The Dragon's Head has been moving through your third room of communication, expression and the talent since October 2001. Its purpose has been to bring forth a certain talent that your soul came in with. This talent has been working to come through and express itself to the world. Saturn has been transiting through the sign of Gemini, through this area of your life, also. Saturn presented your toughest lessons to you through one very close to you. It all had to do with communication. Your natural born talent wished to expose itself through another. Did you receive your reflection? Did you realize what your soul was 'trying' to communicate to you through another? If not, think back on your toughest events of last year and there you will find your soul.

Planetary energies (Venus, Neptune, Uranus and Mercury) are all lining up in your room of friends and social, in the sign of Aquarius. A time for you to show the world what you have been working on is about to present itself to you. Planetary energies are on your side. Many people will like what you have done and are doing. Yet, there will be those who do not. You must realize that it is your certainty that matters. You will attract your fears to you one after the other. Just be certain and clear about what you are doing. If you are having any doubt at all, know that this doubt will be reflected to you through another. Don't just thing it's good, know it is!

This is an incredible time of receiving and attracting opportunities to yourself through others, that is, if your representation of the self in its highest. I can't stress this enough. I am totally exhausted from hearing people say how broke they are. Well, you what being broke is really about? It's about a broken identity. Take a look at those who are strong in their identity. Take a look at those who are confident in their being. Take a look at those who are rich and successful. Do you really think they were all born this way? No. Somewhere along the path of their soul, they decided to work hard and be who they are in their absolute highest. And from just being you and being the best you can be, you will receive in the highest. So just remember, the next time you decide to complain about having no money, know that you are telling yourself and the world that you have no identity.

(February 2003)

TAURUS
APR. 20 - MAY 20

Taurus, you are the sign who represents health, strength, medicine, food, exercise, healing, and so on. You are the care of the land, the care of the physical body. Are you walking in your truth?

This is a time for you to make a decision. Planetary energies are lining up in your tenth room of career, your place / position in the world. It is time for you to acknowledge who you are and become one with this.

Someone will come along and suggest an idea to you. This idea is the thing to catapult you into your place, and a beautiful place it is. However there is fear; fear of trusting another. Do you know that when we have a problem trusting another, it is actually a sign of not trusting the self? You may want to examine your own standards before you judge another's.

This is an excellent time of increasing your monetary cash flow, that is, if you allow yourself to walk your true path. And just how does one find their true path? See a psychic astrologer. That's what we're here for; to assist all in finding and aligning with their true path.

Planetary energies are pulling you out of the home and into the world. It is time for you to connect and be one with yourself. Some of you will receive a raise at this time. Some of you will step out and open your own business. Some of you will receive an advancement within the career you are already in. Some of you will finally realize just what it is you are to be doing. Yet, all of you will make some kind of advancement in the world through career. Your place, where you belong within this world finally becomes apparent.

Spirit says to let you know that those who you have helped along the way has not gone unnoticed. In fact, many seeds you have planted within others have grown and the fruits are ripe and ready for picking'. Your natural born generosity to assist another is coming back around to you. Remember earlier, the message reads, "Someone will come along and suggest an idea to you. This idea is the thing to catapult you into your place." Well, here is a genuine case of 'what goes around, comes around.' You have helped a lot of people in your day, and the Universe is ready to help you.

(February 2003)

GEMINI
MAY 21 - JUN. 20

Things haven't been easy for you Gemini, I know. Sometimes, it has seemed easier to just give up instead of going on. But, you have stuck with this thing called 'life,' and you're doing a fine job with it.

The Dragon's Head and Saturn have been in your Sun sign for quite some time now. The Dragon's Head moved into Gemini in October of 2001, and Saturn in August of 2000. The Dragon's Head will be complete with its transit through Gemini late March 2003, and Saturn will be complete with its transit through Gemini in June 2003. You see, things are getting much better.

You know, the higher lesson of the Dragon's Head and Saturn moving through your Sun sign was to improve you. The Dragon's Head highlighted you to yourself, and Saturn picked out and magnified all of your imperfections. I know it wasn't easy, yet you made it through. Now you should be feeling a lot better about yourself. A feeling of confidence will now radiate through your physical being, for you have perfected your self. Something we all want to do.

Partnership and close relationships have been a very big issue for Gemini in the last year. This is because the Dragon's Tail has been sweeping through your seventh room of partnership. This has been a time for you to see yourself through others and allow a more perfect you to come forth. I am sure many times you have felt as if you were just not good enough for anyone. Well, now a feeling of confidence will overcome you as Saturn makes it way out of your Sun sign. You will see a new and much better you each time you look into the mirror. Mars will cross Pluto this month, in your area of career. Some of you will decide to end the relationship you are presently in, creating a space for a new one to come in. Realize that all you went through with the one you are / were with was indeed a karmic clearing.

An opportunity to do some traveling through your career is likely to take place this month, or perhaps you are offered a job or work assignment in another state. Either way, this looks to be a very good thing. Many of you have waited a while for a change to present itself to you through your career, well, now it's here. Prepare to leave your present surroundings, for a new journey approaches.

(February 2003)

CANCER
JUN. 21 - JUL. 22

Spirit came forth to me and said, "Cancers are givers. They are the assistants to man." I know each one of you have visualized yourself doing something for you. Yet, you know what? This is for you.

In the original astrology, you are the sign that represents the giver and debt payer to society. Now, don't take this negatively, for it is a very positive thing. The Debt Payer is one who has lived many lifetimes where others have assisted you along your path. Spirit says, now you have become a successful one, ready and willing to assist those who assisted you at one time or another. This is actually a joy. Right now, planetary activity is heavily moving through your eighth room of Debts. This is a time where you will receive a vision of who you are and what you are here to do. You are here to give advice. You are here to assist others along the way. You are here to assist those who have at one time and another assisted you.

This is a time of repaying debts. Tie up loose ends and take care of any and all that needs to be taken care for your life is about to move in a very different direction. Yet, before this transition can take place positively, you must first clear your karma.

Mars will cross Pluto this month in your area health and the physical body. Our body is our vehicle throughout this lifetime, and within it are things stored from lifetimes ago. These things will be triggered / activated as Mars crosses Pluto, for this planetary transition is letting us know that your physical body is going through an in-depth cleansing.

You are not sick. Your body is unleashing junk from the past.

Saturn and the Dragon's Head are just about complete with their transit through the sign of Gemini. This activity has been taking place in your room of karma. Many of you, in the last two years, got involved in relationships that were karmically related. There was a great deal of junk that needed to be faced and cleared between you and another. Yet, before Saturn and the Dragon's Head are complete, these energies will drop off one more karmic relationship. This will be the beginning of your new journey, and it looks to be a fun one.

(February 2003)

LEO
JUL. 23 - AUG. 22

You are attracting a great deal of assistance to you either from the partner or one who is very close to you. The upcoming New Moon will take place in the sign of Pisces, placing this energy in your room of Sex, Debts and Partner's Resources. This is a grand time for many of you to begin a new relationship with one who is very caring and very nurturing. For those of you who are already in a relationship, you will attract more caring attention to you from the partner. It looks as if you have had to make a few tough choices, however the partner or someone else is right there by your side for comfort.

Uranus, Neptune, Mercury and Venus are all lining up in the sign of Aquarius, which places this energy in your room of Partnership. The partner will be extra chatty this month, due to planet activity taking place in Aquarius, the sign that represents communication. Jupiter is retrograde in your Sun sign which may cause you to feel a little annoyed or edgy. Do your best to be patient and listen. Some very strong ideas will be presented to you through another. You will want to listen.

Saturn returns direct on the 22nd, placing this energy in your room of friends and social. Something will take place this month that may be rather difficult for you to deal with. Looks like the loss of an old friend. With every loss an opening is created for something new to come in. This is why all the planets are lining up directly across from you, letting you know that someone new is coming in, or this could be a great enhancement in the relationship you are already involved in.

Mars will cross Pluto this month in your area of the family members. This planetary energy could signify the loss of pet or a member of the family. Do your best to see this time as a positive time in your life. We are all growing, learning and evolving. And in doing so, we are accepting life's changes much better than we used to. You are the sign of Higher Knowledge. Be the leader in which you are and teach the rest of us how best to handle and deal with the changes that life presents. And also, remember Jupiter is retrograde this month in your Sun sign, causing you to go deep within and find the higher answers to all of your questions. When you receive the answer, be sure to share it with everyone else. This is a very good time to write.

(February 2003)

VIRGO
AUG. 23 - SEPT. 22

Mars will cross Pluto this month in your area of the home as Saturn returns direct in your place of career. There are many changes that will be taking place this month, and most of them will have to do with relationships.

Our next New Moon will take place in your room of partnership and close relationships. You are about to experience a great change in your home with a partner or one close to you, and you will go through a dramatic change in your area of career pertaining to a close relationship / partnership.

Jupiter is moving retrograde through the sign of Leo in your room of karma. Looks like something from the past will reveal itself, both in your personal and professional life. Jupiter retrograde in your room of karma is letting us know that old secrets will come out at this time. Something you find out will cause you to make a few drastic changes in your living situation and in your career.

Planetary energies (Venus, Neptune, Uranus and Mercury) will all line up in your room of health, in the sign of Aquarius, asking you to bring forth your highest communication when dealing with this situation. You know this situation has that has come around to you has something to with something that was said in the past, or possibly not said. Anyway, this old secret is about to come up and out. If you fight it, realize that these energies are in your room of health, and will cause you great stress on the body if they are not released. Just be honest with yourself and others. You'll surely feel a lot better.

After going through this cleansing that is being presented to you by the Universe, many of you will find yourself connecting with someone new. "Out with the old and in with the new." However, this may not last either. Uranus (planet of sudden changes) is headed towards your room of partnership and close relationships, and will cause whatever relationship you get involved in at this time to suddenly go away. Perhaps you need to connect with yourself a little more. What can this hurt? Absolutely nothing. Your home is need of a make over, so perhaps you will want to spend your time there instead of worry about relationships. Just slow down and take it easy for a while, by yourself.

(February 2003)

LIBRA
SEP. 23 - OCT. 22

Social activity has slowed down quite a bit around you. Jupiter, planet of abundance, is moving retrograde through your room of friends and social activity, causing your socialization to be somewhat stagnant at this time. Spirit says this is a time to focus your energy into the home with your loved ones, children and siblings. Looks like there is a younger person around you who needs some attention.

And, speaking of children, planetary energies are making it very possible for you to attract a few more into your life at this time. Whether they are your own or those of another. An opening has been created for you to attract more of them to you. Why? Well, for some of you it's just that time to start a family. For others of you, perhaps you are ready to add on. And still for others, you'll attract someone else's to you. Or perhaps a sibling you haven't seen in a while is about to return. Either way, a time of communicating with your family members is upon you. Perhaps there is a little remembering that needs to take place, and for you, it will come through this area of your life.

Looks like you are about to let someone have it. Libra, you are the sign that represents friends, social and the gathering of many people. Sagittarius is the sign that rules the way you communicate and express your self to others, individually. You are a very opinionated sign, and don't get me wrong, this is very good. This month, Mars will cross Pluto in your third room of communication, possibly activating a release of some very necessary opinions. Truly, you will not want to hold back what needs to be said at this time, for it just may cause you to hurt your throat. Say what needs to be said. By speaking your truth, you are helping someone out of a stuck pattern they may be in. Your words are your healing power. Heal someone by speaking your truth. Free yourself and another from the thoughts that binds. If anyone can do it, you can. Now, we don't want this to come back around another day, right? Stay in your highest.

For the last few years, some of you have gone through extreme relationship situations. Now it is time for you to choose who you really want to be with. The Dragon's Head is about to enter into your eighth room of the partner's resources, making it very possible for you to attract a provider to you. Be certain about what it is you actually want, for you know, you are just about to get it.

(February 2003)

SCORPIO
OCT. 23 - NOV. 21

A final cleansing is about to be performed on your material assets. Pluto moving through Sagittarius has brought forth the lesson of perfecting the individuality. For you Scorpio, it has been in your finances. Pluto has brought forth extreme energies in this area, meaning, at times, I am sure you have received greatly from the Universe through others. Are you paying your bills and clearing your debt? Surely, I hope so. For if you are taking care of all that is necessary, you will have enough left over to do all you want to do. Planetary energies say, pay your bills, clear your debts and allow that block on your soul to be released. So many times we wonder why we can't move out of a certain spot. Well, it's because there is work that needs to be done, and it hasn't been done yet.

A new home, an expansion of space, or maybe an additional room has been added. Planetary energies say you are preparing your home for someone to come in. Could this be a child, or maybe just a guest? Well you know this visit looks to be permanent. Either way, it looks good. Light blues and lots of air exist here.

Jupiter moving retrograde through your tenth room of career says, relax. Focus your energy into the home with the family. Some of you will decide to start a family at this time. Remember, Spirit said the home is being prepared for someone to come in, permanently.

Your life is all about karma, repetition, and doing the same thing over and over again until you get it right. Your prize is personal fulfillment. And once you reach that personal fulfillment, you'll have reached perfection. And when in that moment of perfection, you will have all you desire to have. Don't give up Scorpio, you're just about there.

The Dragon's Tail is about to enter into your Sun sign for 20 months, beginning in April. Get ready for everything about you to totally change. This will be a time of giving up the self and assisting another. Self-absorption must be eliminated. This is a time of taking other people into consideration and assisting them in finding their way. Personal fulfillment will be obtained through helping others. By the time the sweeping of the Tail is complete, a new and much better you will have emerged.

March 2003

(March 2003)

SAGITTARIUS
NOV. 22 - DEC. 21

Sagittarius, this should feel like a month of celebration, for this is the last month for the Dragon's Tail to sweep through your Sun sign. It moves on in April. A sudden burst of energy and excitement will overcome you. You will feel this power most in your home. It's time to do a little redecorating in celebration of the freedom you are about to experience.

However, stop and take a look at yourself in the mirror. How much have you changed in the last two years? Do you like what you see? Are there some last minute changes you would like to make? Go ahead and make them. The purpose of the Dragon's Tail sweeping through your Sun sign was to assist you in releasing the old and the outdated. You should be feeling foot loose and fancy free. A new you have emerged through this two-year transformation, and I say it's time to celebrate.

This looks like a very good month to clean and redecorate the home, and possibly invite a few friends over for a celebration of life party. You really don't need an excuse to celebrate life, now do you?

Because of the stress that has been on personal relationships through Saturn in Gemini, many of you have probably made the decision to withdraw. Saturn continues its transit through your seventh room of partnerships until June of 2003. We're all still going through the issues of trust and difference. Saturn has a way of bringing forth stuff we just don't want to look at and deal with. Yet, you know what? Let's just face it. Let's stare Saturn right in the eyes and let him know how we feel. Just remember, Saturn's job is not to make us mad or angry. Saturn in Gemini is reflecting to us the things we hate most, just so we can face our fears and find the love in the situation. Saturn's job is to assist us in bringing forth our best. I never said this is easy. However, it is something we all have to go through.

Your vibrant energy is attracting all sorts of gifts to you through others. This is the Universe's way of rewarding you for doing such a fine job with yourself. You are lovely.

(March 2003)

CAPRICORN
DEC. 22 - JAN. 20

Minor things concerning your health and overall physical strength may have been bothering you Capricorn. However, Mars, planet of physical strength, power and motivation will be moving through your Sun sign this month, fueling you with a little extra energy. Mars is a healing planet. It's incredible power comes forth and strengthens our body tremendously. Mars moving through your sun sign will definitely bring forth incredible strength, power and motivation to get you through the month. Use this extra energy to do a little redecorating around the house. This is a very good time of year for you to spruce up the home.

Speaking of the home, are you looking for a new one? Planetary energies are making it possible for a new home to come about, or maybe there's some major redecorating you want to do. Either way, a change presents itself in the area of the home.

Spirit says there are some very beautiful and unique gifts that will be coming your way, also, possibly things to assist in sprucing up the home. Yet, you know how it goes. Before we can receive what is destined to come our way, we must make room for it to come in. If there are things that need to go, let them go. Make room in your personal world for beautiful things to find their way to you.

Uranus moves into the sign of Pisces this month, placing it in your third room of communication and expression. Is there writing you are wanting to do, or perhaps painting or drawing? Capricorns make great designers, whether you are designing a home, a wall, an office or a particular room, or maybe you're designing clothes or someone's face? Anyway, this is a very good time to start a new project.

Uranus makes things happen suddenly, quickly and unexpectedly. Get ready for a particular talent to burst from within. Now, don't get all upset if the feeling doesn't stick. Uranus will go retrograde (which means relaxed) in June. So therefore, this burst of energy and motivation will come and will go. Do not try and force anything to be before its time. Just move with the flow, relax and enjoy life.

(March 2003)

AQUARIUS
JAN. 21 - FEB. 18

Uranus moved into the sign of Aquarius in April of 1995 and has been there since. Uranus is the planet of sudden change, growth and expansion. Uranus' energy comes in and breaks down our false structure, presenting a chance for us to rebuild and redo. For you Aquarius, Uranus has been moving through your sun sign, breaking down all that has had to do with your outer appearance that has not really been you. Uranus prepares to move out of your sun sign this month on the 10th. The unfolding of you takes place.

A new you awakens. You have prepared long and hard for this moment, going through your back and forth, trying on new masks and identities, only to find that most of them weren't you in the first place. Now, look at you. Uranus moves on leaving behind this incredible new person. Truly, I hope you like what you see.

Neptune continues its transit through your Sun sign. Neptune's job moving through your first room of Self is to enhance who you have now become. Neptune will take this new you to a much higher level. You have it made.

All these years, you have walked along side someone else, boosting up their ego and self-confidence. Now, it is your turn. Finally, who you really are has come into form and can now walk proudly amongst the face of this planet, and say "I Am." Can you feel it? You have become one with yourself and everyone around you knows it. I am proud of you Aquarius. You have gone through a most intense and most incredible transformation.

Uranus enters into your second room of material receiving this month. The Universe is about to reward you for work done well. The work Spirit is talking about, is the work you have done on / with yourself. Uranus makes things happen suddenly, quickly and unexpectedly. Just remember. As quick as things come in, so will they go out. During this time of Uranus transiting your second room of material possessions, try not to hold on to anything. Enjoy everything and all within the moment. When it is time to release, let it go. There is always more to come. Uranus will transit this area of your life from now until April 2011.

(March 2003)

PISCES
FEB. 19 - MAR. 19

Pisces, Uranus steps into your Sun sign this month, and will be there until March 2011. Uranus is the planet of sudden change and erratic activity. Uranus comes in and breaks down false structure, so that something new can be rebuilt.

For the next more than few years, your personal identity will go through a complete makeover. By the end of the Uranus transit, a totally new you will have emerged. Uranus will take you through a karmic cleansing of who you used to be, just so who you are born to be within this lifetime may come forth.

Uranus has come into your life to get rid of everything false that is attached to you; your hair color, your make-up, the clothes you wear and so on. You are about to go through a complete transformation of the self. The true essence of the soul prepares to reveal itself to the world. Get ready Pisces. This transformation starts off gentle, for Venus is right there by Uranus' side. However, Venus moves on, and Uranus will linger.

A new talent is about to present itself through a young male who presents a gift to you. This gift looks to have something to do with children. This gift can turn into a moneymaking venture if you allow it. This gift is the revelation of what you are to do next.

The Dragon's Tail has been sweeping through your 10th area of Career since October 2001. Your place / standing within this world has gone through an intense cleansing. Who are you and why are you here have been the questions your mind has been asking for quite some time. Now, the answer to those questions is revealed. Pay attention to the young male who crosses your path, for this young male will have the answer you seek.

Your body and physical energy may go through a lack of. You may find your energy level down, and possibly wanting to sleep a little more than usual. Go with the flow. If your body is calling for additional rest, then by all means, give it what it needs.

(March 2003)

ARIES
MAR. 20 - APR. 19

You are in preparation for the birth of a new you, your birthday.

Something you have been fighting with finally shows some progress. I also see that your fight with your Self is just about over.

In August of 2000, Saturn moved into the sign of Gemini, which placed it is your third room of communication and expression. The third room is also the room of our creative talent, our unique gift. Saturn in Gemini has worked to reveal your talent through one very close to you. Yet, sometimes, when things are right up in our face, we usually don't recognize them. However, I feel you will.

You are finally coming into the realization of who you are and your place in this world. Mars moves into the sign of Capricorn this month (money) in your tenth room of Career. CHARGE!!! This is your time of connecting and becoming one with who you are.

Spirit says to tell you that listening is a very important factor in your life. Pluto continues to transit through your ninth room of Higher Knowledge. Pluto in Sagittarius says "Perfect Individual." This means one. There is one person in your life at this time that represents 'perfect individuality' to you. This person will reveal your soul. This person has been sent into your life, according to plan, to assist you in discovering whom you are. If your ego thinks it knows everything already, you will surely miss out on this grand opportunity to 'know thyself.' Remember to LISTEN to this one. And let there be one, because there is one.

Jupiter prepares itself to return direct next month. Jupiter is the planet of abundance, and right now, Jupiter is transiting your fifth room of children. An opening will be created for many children to come into your life. Use this message as a warning. Prepare your foundation now, for a multitude of little ones are coming for a visit, and this visit may be permanent. So therefore, the better you prepare your world, the better you will do with this incredible force.

Uranus has moved into your room of karma for the next eight years. Prepare for an intense karmic awakening to occur.

(March 2003)

TAURUS
APR. 20 - MAY 20

Taurus, you are the builder and healer of the earth.

In the last two years, many people have crossed your path with many ideas. You were presented an opportunity to have your own place of business. Some of you passed the test of Neptune moving through your Career, and some of you did not. What is the test of Neptune? The test of Neptune in Aquarius is communication in its highest. Neptune's transit through your area of career says "yes" you will receive greatly as long as what you present what 'is' exactly how it is.

The test of Neptune in Aquarius in your tenth room of Career says communication and representation in the absolute highest in order to attract this grand business opportunity to you. This grand business opportunity was a chance to be in your own business, brought about by another, a business investor. However, some of you did not use the energies of Neptune in their highest. For those who did, congratulations!

For those of you who are walking in your highest, you are now in a very successful moving business for yourself. Many nurturing and assertive people will be coming into your life, one after the other, to assist you with your wonderful business you have created for the world. Your business is a place of healing for all. You have aligned with your purpose. Spirit says a dream has become reality for some of you. Continue to walk in your highest, and you will continue to receive in the highest.

The Dragon's Tail is about to enter into your seventh room of partnership and close relationships as the Dragon's Head moves into your first room of self. Many of you will go through a divorce, separation or detachment of some kind or another. This is a time of learning to stand alone, on your own two feet. An idea has become apparent and has created a place for you in the world. Someone has come along to support this idea and to assist you in getting it started. Now that this energy is in place, it is now time for you to carry it on alone. Remember, this is your test of the individuality. This is your lesson of learning to stand on your own two feet

(March 2003)

GEMINI
MAY 21 - JUN. 20

Your friends are young, fun and full of life, and it looks like you are about to connect with a few new ones. Have you ever wondered why you seem to attract child-like individuals into your life? Well, it's the Aries energy that exists in your eleventh room of friends. Spirit says that this is also a very good time for you to get out of the house and enjoy yourself. Time to have some fun and get a little exercise while you're at it.

Gemini's do well to get involved in a career where they are caring for others. You are such a one-on-one energy and you connect extremely well with the needs of others. Uranus, planet of sudden change and erratic activity, moves into the sign of Pisces this month, which places its energy into your tenth room of Career. Uranus is about to break down whatever you have built up, giving you a chance to rebuild.

Spirit says that many of you are in professions that truly have nothing to do with your character. As Uranus makes its way through your tenth room of career, this will all change. Your profession / place within this world is about to go through a major change and restructuring. Whatever you have been doing up to this point is all about to change, and for the better.

Difficulties with personal relationships are about to cease. The Dragon's Tail prepares to transition from your seventh room of partnership, however, Pluto remains. Pluto is energy of death, transformation and perfection. Pluto will remain in your seventh room of partnership until late January of 2008. For those of you whose relationships made it though the sweeping of the Dragon's Tail, your partner is about to go through an incredible transformation. Yes, that's right! Your partner is finally about to get his / her stuff together. I know it has been tough dealing with someone who has had a lack of funds and character, but guess what? This is all about to change. I know many relationships did not make it last year, for the transition of Pluto and the Dragon's Tail were hard aspects to deal with. Well, now the Dragon's Tail is moving on. Pluto transiting through your seventh room of Partnership will actually assist in enhancing the personality and character of your partner. He / She is about to become the best person he / she can possibly be at this time. And believe me, there is a reward in this for you, too. Just hang in there.

(March 2003)

Remember earlier in the year, Spirit spoke of one last person coming into your life just before the Dragon moved out of the sign of Gemini. Well here comes that person. Mars will move into your room of partnership this month as the upcoming New Moon and Mercury transit through your room of career. This person who will be entering into your life is the one your soul has promised to be with at this time. All you need to do is be in the right place at the right time. And just how is one in the right place at the right time? By following his instincts.

Through this one you are destined to connect with is also a new career. Many of you will begin a new career this month and meet this person there. Also connected to this new relationship is lots of travel. You may even find yourself revisiting your home. This 'home' could also be symbolic of a familiar place of the soul.

Extreme joy and comfort will run through your veins, intoxicating your senses to the point where you will feel as if this is not real. Oh yes! This is real.

The Dragon moves on next month, placing its head in your eleventh room of friends and social and its tail in your fifth room of family members. Get ready for planetary energies to pull you to the outside world. Your spirit wants to be free and expressive, and one way for the soul to acknowledge itself to the mind is to attract one just like it before you. And sometimes, the only way for us to see our self through another is to step outside of the home and experience. You are about to attract a lot of wonderful people your way. Many of who will be giving you a direct reflection of your soul. You are about to meet your true self.

Saturn, lord of karma, continues to transit through your twelfth room of karma, in the sign of Gemini. Saturn has been confusing your thoughts for the last two years. If you have wondered why it has been so difficult for you to make up your mind, know it is Saturn. Saturn's energy will also bring about depression, causing you to go deep within the self so that you may come face-to-face with your true identity. Get ready Cancer. Your soul is about to expose itself to the world.

(March 2003)

LEO
JUL. 23 - AUG. 22

Your energies are very positive these days, however, it looks as if you continue to attract a few miserably deceiving people to you. Relax. This energy is all about to change. Spirit says that these people are reflections of your past. Spirit asks that you just see yourself in what you are attracting. Do your best to detach from judgment and try to move on. There is really no need to hang on to what someone else has said or done.

It looks as if you are about to receive news from away. Someone who does not live in the same area as you will be calling to tell you about a personal transformation they have gone through. Something they say will remind you of yourself. Once again, allow you to see yourself through someone else. Looks like you'll be doing some remembering of your childhood. Planetary energies also suggest a little traveling this month, perhaps to visit a family member. Don't talk yourself out of this again. Go. There's a whole lot more to gain than just a visit.

And just what is the higher purpose of this remembering? Well, as the Dragon's Tail has transited your fifth room of children / siblings through the last two years. Many events that took place in your life, especially those pertaining to younger people, stirred up old memories of when you were a child. This has been a time of remembering your childhood and clearing old issues of the past, because it is time to move on. You are evolving to a higher level, and in order for the new to come through, the old must go. And in order for the old to go, the past must be faced, dealt with and released.

Jupiter is moving through your Sun sign, expanding your identity and character to the world. A more powerful you prepare to expose. And through the sweeping of the Dragon's Tail in your fifth room of children, you are clearing whatever needs to be cleared at this time, just so a more powerful you may emerge.

As far as partnership and close relationships go, it looks as if you will be attracting more of a helping hand to you from your partner. All of a sudden, the partner assists like never before. Incredible! What have you done to deserve this?

(March 2003)

VIRGO
AUG. 23 - SEPT. 22

All of a sudden, you will attract to you energy from your partner; the kind of attention you have wanted to attract for years. What is it, and why now? Beautiful Venus and Uranus will be side by side in your seventh room of partnership, suddenly bringing forth to you a loving, considerate, and nurturing partner. You are finally attracting to you what you have wanted for a very long time. And that's not all. You and this person look as if you may be going into some kind of business with one another. This is exactly what this time has been all about. And just what time am I talking about? Well, The Dragon's Head has been moving through the sign of Gemini for the last year and a half, in your tenth room of Career. The purpose of the Dragon's Head in this area of your life was to bring forth a partner whom your soul was destined to be with and work with. Now, it finally all comes together. Saturn has also been transiting through the sign of Gemini since August of 2000. Saturn has made it very difficult for you to see the connection between you and this person, for there was a lot of karmic junk to clear. It all makes sense.

Every Virgo I know has gone through the most incredible transformations in the area of partnerships and close relationships. And I have told you all, "hang in there, you're clearing karma. As soon as the karma is cleared, there is a beautiful love, work and play relationship that will come about. Yet, first, you'll have to clear the karmic junk." Planetary energies are now showing me that what Spirit has been telling me all along is finally coming into place.

Some of you may get involved in a new relationship at this time. Well, if you do, know that this is a soul connection, for the Dragon's Head is still in Gemini. Also know that this person may have children, for the energy of Mars transits your fifth room of children. Yet, most importantly, know that this person is full of life, play, love, care, tenderness and money. Yep, that's right! This person whom you are attracting to you has quite a bit of money, too, and isn't stingy. Wow!

Many of you went through changes in the home last month and late last year. The final touches remain. If there is any other clearing that needs to be done, do so now. For a brand new life has presented itself to you, and it looks absolutely incredible.

(March 2003)

LIBRA
SEP. 23 - OCT. 22

An opening occurs in your area of partnership and close relationships. Someone comes into your life with a somewhat young vibration. This doesn't look like a child, however, this person does have a child-like personality. So, what is the purpose of someone coming into your life right now? Well, for many reasons. First of all, for those of who are not married or in a committed relationship, one is about to form. The Dragon's Head has been transiting through the sign of Gemini in your ninth room of Higher Knowledge since October of 2001. The purpose of this transit was to create an opening for you to attract your soul mate. Your soul mate is very intelligent, very knowledgeable and a traveler. This alignment of the two souls is destined to take place at this time, for you and this other will go on a journey together to create and build something together.

Mars will be moving through your home this month, providing you with the power and motivation to get rid of and throw out any and all that is no longer necessary for your spiritual growth. A cleansing needs to be performed in your home. Cleansing helps to keep us young, vibrant and healthy. Cleansing keeps us from holding on to stuff that are no longer needed. We are here to live life in the fullest, and in order to do this we must keep our energy free and clear of clutter. Clutter weighs us down and keeps us from moving freely. Release all can at this time, and prepare for a new journey to begin.

Neptune continues its transit through your room of children until April 2011. Neptune is the planet of high illusions, daydreams, secrets and the unknown. Neptune is also the power and ability to go beyond the physical. Right now, you are receiving a lesson from Neptune through your children. What are they really doing? What's really going on in their life? Think back on when you were a child and the things you did that you cared not to share with your parents. Know that this same thing has come around to show you as the parent what it feels like. Or perhaps, you don't have any children. What about your siblings, or your closest friends? Have you been a deceiving person in your day? Have you done a little secret talking about another? Just know that this energy has come back around and will treat you the same way you have treated another. The positive side of Neptune is higher vision, higher sight, and one very close to God. There will be at least one like this around you. Learn as much as you can.

(March 2003)

SCORPIO
OCT. 23 - NOV. 21

The Dragon's Tail has been sweeping through your second room of material possessions since October 2001, assisting you in getting rid of a lot of stuff. This has been a time of clearing for you. Personal belongings that you have held on to need to be released in order for you to grow in the way you are destined to grow. It is time to remove the physical / material layers. Clearing out your closets, going through old boxes and storage. Emptying drawers and whatever else has been storing things. Use this final time of the Dragon's Tail sweeping through your second room to finally get rid of all that stuff you have been holding onto for years. It's time to release your load, for a time approaches where you will be on the go.

Uranus enters into your fifth room of children / siblings. Uranus is so unpredictable, like lightening. You never know where it's going to strike. Uranus moving through this area of your life concentrates on a young female at this time. There is quite a bit of attention this young woman will need from you. There is a specific learning you are to receive at this time through this other.

Neptune continues its transit through your fourth room of home. Neptune of the physical is secrets and the unknown. Beware of certain activities going on around you in your home that may be in secret. There will be many times, however, where this unknown will unfold.

Planetary energies suggest that this is a pretty big time for you too. Once again, concentrate your energies into the home, clean it and rebuild it if necessary. Pay close attention to your children / siblings and make sure you are doing all that is necessary to be done. Leave no stone unturned. Go through every detail within this area of your life. For come next month, Jupiter returns direct in your tenth room of career and you will find yourself very busy and constantly on the road. Spirit says that this is the time for you to make sure that your home and children are fine, strong and stable, for planetary energies are about to pull you away from this area of your life for a while. And the only way you can enjoy what is about to take place with your life is to make sure that the opposite of this area is finely tuned. Clear your closets, release the old, fine tune the energies in your home, and get ready for the new to come in.

April 2003

(April 2003)

SAGITTARIUS
NOV. 22 - DEC. 21

The Dragon's Tail will enter into the sign of Scorpio this month, placing this energy in your room of karma and spirituality. The Dragon's Head will enter into the sign of Taurus, placing its energy into your room of health and the physical body. You are about to go through and experience an extensive karmic cleansing. Everything your soul has gone through within the lifetime of your soul is about to be expressed through your physical body. No, this will not be an easy time for any of you, however, know that your Divine God and Goddess are right beside you to guide you along the way.

I know many of you will feel as if you have already gone through as much as you feel you can take. Well, there is more. This is not meant to be a time of hardship or sorrow. This is a time of cleansing. This is a time of clearing all that is insignificant with the will of your soul. Do your best to not fight with this transformation you are going through, for it will not last long. This cleansing of your spiritual closet will be complete late December 2004. All you need to know and realize is that your soul is now going through a complete cleansing. Just go along with the flow.

You are born a Sagittarius. Sagittarius is the sign that represents individuality, oneness, leadership, management and the ability to stand as one. You are a powerful person, and in order for this incredible power to come forth, something incredible must take place to release it. Christ walked as a Sagittarian (complete individual) as so did the Buddha. All great leaders represent and demonstrate the power of the individuality. Now, it is your turn. Know that the planetary energy of Pluto in your Sun sign, and the sweeping of the Dragon's Tail in Scorpio, are both working to clear your world of what no longer needs to be there, so that your true essence may be exposed.

Mercury goes retrograde at the end of the month in your room of health. Rest, pray and meditate. Your spirit is trying to communicate with your mind.

(April 2003)

CAPRICORN
DEC. 22 - JAN. 20

An issue of taking care of a child, or someone who is like a child approaches, and this situation is related to health. Planetary energies also suggest that the desire to care for this individual is low. This situation you are in is something you have intensely asked for, and now that you have it, you're not sure you want it. Isn't it funny how life just seems to keep repeating itself? You would think you would have learned by now.

Money plays a very big role in this situation you are in. Could this be the reason you are in the situation you are in? I am sure this has a lot to do with it.

For those of you Capricorns who are walking in your highest, this can actually be a very positive time in your life. Money and material means seem to be flowing abundantly your way, all because you are unselfishly doing what you are to be doing.

The Dragon's Tail has moved into your eleventh room of Friends and Social, eliminating all whom you have been connected with, pulling your energies into the home where it is needed at this time.

Basically, it looks like your life has been severely altered because of a choice you made some time ago. Now, all you can do is your best. Times will approach where you will feel as if you don't want to continue on doing what you are doing, however, Spirit says, do your best and be your best. This and only this is what will release you from the karma you have created for yourself. Just do your best.

Your own health will begin to take its toll if you allow it. Spirit says to tell you, once again, that this situation you have called upon yourself is indeed one you have asked, wished and begged for. Now that you have it, enjoy it. Do the best you can possibly do with this situation, for one day, you will receive your just reward. May the Gods love, bless and keep you well at this very karmic time in your life.

(April 2003)

AQUARIUS
JAN. 21 - FEB. 18

A new life, a new home, a new job, a new relationship and a new you are finally coming into order. Uranus has briefly moved out of your Sun sign, the Dragon's Tail will begin sweeping through your room of Career (place within this world) and the Dragon's Head will transit your room of Home / Mother.

The Dragon's Tail has now entered into the sign of Scorpio, in your room of the Career / Father. Many of you will go through the transformation of the father as the Dragon's Tail sweeps through this area. Many of you will go through the transformation of your career. Many of you will go through a clearing of both. Scorpio is the sign that rules your Career (place within this world). Scorpio is the sign of karma, that from the past. Most Aquarian souls have come in with a direct path to do something that they wanted to do in a previous lifetime. If you do not remember what this is, go back to when you were a child. What did you see yourself doing? This will assist you in remembering the true path of your soul. As the Dragon's Tail sweeps through this area of your life for the next twenty months, this path will be revealed to you.

The Dragon's Head will move into the sign of Taurus this month, placing this energy in your room of the Home / Mother. Many of you are about to move into a new home. Many of you are about to find yourself caring for a parent. Many of you will find yourself doing exactly what your soul has come here to do. Aquarius is the sign that rules Speech, Communication and Expression. You are the sign that rules the talent. Get ready Aquarius for your true talent to expose itself. This may be something you will do from the home, for the energy of Taurus that exists there indicates stability.

Jupiter, planet of abundance, returns to direct mode this month, in the sign of Leo, placed in your room of partnership and close relationships. Jupiter transiting through this area indicates marriage or the solidifying of a relationship. Many of you will connect with a new relationship at this time, one who is highly intelligent, loves to read, is somewhat sociable, and loves to travel.

(April 2003)

PISCES
FEB. 19 - MAR. 19

The Dragon's Tail swept through your tenth room of Career (your place in the world) for the last year and a half. The message of the Tail was for you to find your unique individuality through this transition. For those of you who did allow yourself to move with the flow of energy, you are now standing in your unique oneness and individuality. In this area of Career, there were many challenges to tend to, and most of those were between you and one other. Yet, now it has passed. The energies have moved on and you are now to free to do as you need to do in another area of your life, which looks to be in the area of education.

Spirit says, that what you 'think' you may need to know and learn at this time, is already there. Scorpio, the sign of karma and the past, is the energy that rules your ninth room of Higher Knowledge and Education. The Dragon's Tail has now entered into this area of your life, sweeping through the knowledge and information that is already contained within you, bringing it up and out and through to the physical. Spirit says that in order for your mind to receive this higher knowledge that is already contained within you, you must allow yourself to thoroughly cleanse the physical body. Prepare the physical to receive the spiritual. The spiritual is the higher order. It is the energy and the purpose of life. Spirit says, prepare a space within your life to allow your spirit to do as it has come upon this earth to do.

Uranus has moved into your Sun sign for the next eight years. Uranus is the planet of high energy, erratic activity, and sudden and quick change. Prepare yourself to go through the most intense outer transformations you have yet had to go through. Spirit says that first your body will take on the appearance of past lifetime forms, one at a time. As you reconnect with each past lifetime, one at a time, it will be released and you will move on to the next one, until you return to your original self. Uranus moving through your Sun sign is removing the mask, bit by bit, exposing your true identity. This is a very powerful time in ones life. Embrace it.

(April 2003)

ARIES
MAR. 20 - APR. 19

All of that hard work you have put into whatever it is you are working on, is about to pay off. The Dragon's Head officially moves into your second room of material gain and receiving this month. Whatever gift or talent exposed itself to you last year is now ready to flourish, and this is your month of celebration. However, there is still a little fine-tuning that will need to be done.

One of your major lessons in life has been listening. Pluto has been moving through your ninth room of Higher Knowledge since January of 1995. Think back through this time and remember all you have gone through. Every situation you attracted to yourself since then has all had to do with you discovering your highest self through knowledge. There were many times where you 'thought' you knew best, and chose not to listen. And from this rebellious attitude, there were many times when you fell and found it difficult to get up. Now, there are younger ones around you whom you see doing this very exact thing. Not listening and thinking they know better than you. What goes around comes around. Don't get mad, which is one thing Aries people are very good at. See the reflection in this situation. The same way you needed to learn it for yourself (no matter what anyone had to say, let these younger people who are around you do the same. Let them learn it for themselves and quit telling other's what they should or should not do.

Last year, planetary energies lined up heavily in your third room of communication and expression. A talent was born. A higher discovery of the Self revealed itself to you. Saturn is the only planet that continues to linger in this area of your life, fine-tuning and perfecting this gift of the self. Saturn moves on in June. No matter what it was that you discovered of yourself, if you listened and perfected every step, you will receive fantastically. Use these final days to call forth Saturn's energy to assist you in perfecting the finishing touches. Believe me, it will make a very big difference in what is about to happen next. Whatever talent exposed itself to you last year, use this time to make it even better. Perfect it one step further.

(April 2003)

TAURUS
APR. 20 - MAY 20

The Dragon's Head will officially move into your first room of Self and the Tail will move into your seventh room of Partnership. The Dragon's Tail indicates that a sweeping / cleansing has now begun in the area of partnership and close relationships. The Dragon's Tail is sweeping through the sign of Scorpio. Scorpio is the sign of karma and the past. The Dragon's Tail sweeping through the sign of Scorpio in your seventh room partnership and close relationships says that things that have been kept or hidden from you are about to reveal. Whatever close relationship you are in at this time, a cleansing is occurring. This may also be a time where you will want to sever the relationship because of the difficulty you may have dealing with what has been kept from you. Of course, this is your choice. Just remember there are things about you, also, that one day will be exposed.

The Dragon's Head moves into the sign of Taurus, transiting your first room of Self. Your outer appearance is about to go through great changes. An enhancement of the identity takes place as the Dragon's Head transits your first room of Self.

Your individuality is about to go through a test of character. The Universe is making is possible for you to attract someone to you who will fund an idea you have. However, considering the planetary activity that is taking place directly across from you, you may decide to allow this opportunity to go on by. Spirit says, do not allow your false judgments to cloud this situation. Your judgment of another's character is the judgment of yourself. There may be many things that you will not like about this individual, however, know this individual is a direct reflection of you. This opportunity you are attracting to you is your ability to finally express what you have wanted to express for some time. Now is your chance. Your personal judgments of this other person may keep you from expressing your talent in the way in which it is meant. Just know what it is you are actually judging.

You are in preparation to go to the next level of your life (birthday). Use this time to meditate, pray and envision what it is you desire to achieve within this next year.

(April 2003)

GEMINI
MAY 21 - JUN. 20

Looks like there may be a lot on your mind these days. Do you desire a change or have you been thinking about moving or relocating? Well, planetary energies suggest a change is on its way. However, I feel your mind must first come into alignment with what your soul is here to do. The journey of the soul is always a positive one. The only thing that makes life a struggle is our resistance to it. Anyway, a few tough choices are on their way. The reason the choice will be tough is because of that thing called the battle between mind and spirit. Also known as the battle between darkness and light, good and evil, God and the Devil. Truly, it is all in your mind. Clear your mind and you clear the battle.

Saturn continues to move through your Sun sign this month, continuing to take your thoughts through those typical back and forth. Truly, it is time you get used to it. You're a Gemini. Throughout your entire lifetime, you will go back and forth with everything that comes your way. It's not necessarily to choose one way or the other; it's all about balance. Allowing the masculine and feminine energies to work as one.

Your thoughts are rambling and your mouth is likely to do so also. Perhaps you'll want to take up a new hobby or something. Considering how the planets are moving around and about for you, it's not going to be easy deciding 'what' you want to do. Anyway, there's a female friend around who looks to be a lot of fun and will actually help to balance out your thoughts.

As far as personal relationships go, Pluto continues its transit through this area of your life until late January of 2008. Pluto is the planet of God / Perfection. Your relationships will go back and forth as Pluto transits here. One moment, it will seem absolutely perfect. The next moment, it will seem absolutely unbearable. This is Pluto going direct and then retrograde and you will have this to deal with until January of 2008. The whole purpose of this transit is to show you the absolute best and the absolute worst. You know the old saying, "For better and worse, richer and poorer."

(April 2003)

The Dragon's Head moves into your eleventh room of Friends and Social this month and the following New Moon will join it. This month, you will receive a vision of where you are to be and what you are to be doing through other people. Some of you may already know your place, so therefore you will receive a vision on how you can improve your already existing 'thing."

Even though this is a very good month to be surrounded by your friends and to do lots of socializing, Mercury will go stationary and then retrograde in this same area, causing you to feel a little confused with the visions you receive. There is no hurry to make a definite decision about anything. Mercury going retrograde says, relax your mind and allow your thoughts to move slowly and fine tune whatever it is that's in your head. Mercury going retrograde is actually a very positive thing, however, many fear it. Once in a while, we need to slow down and fine tune. Most of us are racing around and hurriedly trying to get from one place to another. Mercury retrograde says, "Hey, wait a minute. Slow down, take your time and think this through a little more." So you see. Even though planetary energies suggest that a grand idea is about to present itself to you, you don't have to make a definite decision about it right away.

Cancer, later this month, you will be approached by a person who has an idea about something they want to do. This idea will be presented to you because you are the perfect assistant. This idea will also include travel, finding yourself going from here to there. Because the Dragon's Tail has now entered into your room of family members, you may find yourself far from home, and somewhat detached from your family. This is a part of your soul's plan. However, since Mercury will go retrograde later this month, planetary energies do suggest that you will delay in making a decision. This is good. Taking your time in making this decision is indeed the correct thing to do while Mercury moves in retrograde.

Anyway, prepare yourself for a wonderful life change. You are about to discover many different sides of yourself through this journey.

(April 2003)

LEO
JUL. 23 - AUG. 22

Jupiter, planet of abundance, returns direct this month in your Sun sign. You will begin to feel yourself coming back into alignment with your full power. Jupiter will also bless you with the power of attraction. Put forth your absolute best with all that you do, for through the things you do, you will attract something else. Depending upon 'what' type of power you put forth depends on what you attract to you.

The Dragon's Tail will move into the sign of Scorpio this month, placing this energy in your fourth room of the Home / Mother. Many of you will go the loss of a nurturing figure in your life as the Tail sweeps through this area of your life. Many of you will go through a sudden change in residence. Yet, the main lesson here is clearing. Clearing your old karmic issues you have related to the mother and your childhood.

Planetary energies are suggesting that a very big opening is taking place within this world, and all for you. Who are you this day? Who do you wish to become? How do you wish the world to remember you? It's never to late to begin. Clear your old issues related to the mother, the home you grew up in and your childhood. This is what this time is all about. A very good way to clear old thoughts is to write them down on paper and then to burn the paper. Just give it a try.

There will be a young male coming into your life this month, a very creative one. This young male figure is one from one of your previous past lifetimes. Your mission is to assist him along his path. This young male will be extremely creative and expressive. He is a reflection of you. Putting yourself in this young mans shoes, what would you want someone to do for you? Your answer to this question is exactly what you are meant to do for him. This young male possess an incredible talent, one your soul is destined to promote and expose to the world. Leo, you are the sign that represents higher knowledge, education and information. This young male has come to you for this. This young male is a duplicate of you somewhere in your life. Helping him is helping you. Attempt to see your reflection.

(April 2003)

VIRGO
AUG. 23 - SEPT. 22

The Dragon's Tail will enter into the sign of Scorpio (karma), sweeping through your area of the talent. The many wants and desires of the soul are about to expose themselves you, one at a time. Just before the Tail completes its transit in this area of your life, you true destiny will have exposed itself. The Dragon's Tail will sweep through this area of your life from now until late December 2004.

Many of you Virgos are about to go through a beautiful move / relocation. The Dragon's Head enters into your ninth room of travel, as Pluto continues its transit through your home. These two planetary aspects say change, move and relocation. Uranus, planet of sudden change, is now transiting through your seventh room of Partnership, letting us know that this change will have much to do with a relationship you are now in.

Uranus, planet of sudden change and activity is now transiting your seventh room of partnership and close relationships. Many relationships will end under this transit, making room for new ones to begin. New relationships that begin under this transit may not last long, for this planetary energy symbolizes a clearing within this area. Once the cleansing of this area is complete, an old relationship may return, however, this will be in eight years. The higher meaning of Uranus transiting through this area is to connect your soul with other souls you have been with in other lifetimes. This is a time of remembering, clearing and releasing. Yet, by the time Uranus is complete with this area, there will be someone left for you. You will go through the lesson of relationships as Uranus transits this area.

Saturn first entered into your room of Career / Father in August of 2000. A very masculine energy presented itself to many of you. Many of you whose souls have been in positions of leadership and authority were faced with one much like you. In other words, many of you received a challenge of attracting one as tough as you. This was karma. King against King. Did you allow your world to align with another's? This was your test / lesson of Saturn in Gemini. Saturn moves on in June.

(April 2003)

LIBRA
SEP. 23 - OCT. 22

Your life has been preparing to be joined with that of another. The Dragon's Head moves into your eighth room of the Partner's Resources as the Tail will sweep through your second room of personal belongings. Yes, that is right. This time presents a moment of getting rid of your own and assisting another with their thing. Libra is the sign that represents many people, friends and social activities. You are a natural promoter by the birth of your soul. Your entire life focuses on bringing the people "to-gather" for one social event after the other. This person who your soul is destined to connect with at this time is one of great energy, youth and motivation. This person was presented an idea last year, and is now preparing to manifest this idea, and with your help and assistance. Are you willing? Many things you have been asking your Guides for, many things you are wanting, many things you are wanting to do are all connected to you following out this destined plan with this individual. Many of you may have things you want to do for yourself, yet this does not mean you cannot. Helping another serves the self. See how you are to assist this other person with his / her life. For believe me, this person's life has all to do with yours.

Jupiter returns direct this month in your ruling room of Friends and Social. If you allow yourself to connect with this individual idea, you will do your part very well, which is gathering the people. Jupiter in this area of your life says this is a time where many people will come you way for there is something you have, or perhaps something you know, and this multitude of people will want to gather around you to see what it is.

As I said earlier, the Dragon's Tail will now enter into your second room of material possessions. It is time for you to get rid of your own stuff. Let it go, for something much better wants to come in. Many of you will connect with one who will take you on a far away journey. This journey could be out of the state, out of the country, out of this world, or out of your mind. And yet, this is all a part of the plan.

(April 2003)

SCORPIO
OCT. 23 - NOV. 21

Your true identity will be revealed as the Dragon's Tail sweeps through your Sun sign for the next 20 months. That's right Scorpio, everything about you is about to go through an intense cleanse. The modern world sees you as a very secretive person. I don't. I see you as one who keeps your junk to yourself. Why is this anyone's business? It's not. The other day as I was driving along the freeway, traffic came to an absolute halt for about three miles. I sat thinking to myself what could be going on up there. As I reached the point of conflict, I saw there had been an accident, yet all accident vehicles were off to the right shoulder of the road. I called out to my guides and said, "Now what is the message here!!!???" I saw absolutely no reason why traffic should move so slowly. Spirit came forth and said, "People in other peoples business slows down the world." One thought led to another and all of a sudden, life began to make a little more sense to me. So you see, what you keep to yourself is absolutely your business. Other's wanting to know what you're up to will only slow them down trying to figure you out. My point is, just be you Scorpio. Just because the Dragon's Tail is about to sweep through your individuality, it does not mean you need to reveal all about you to the world. It means you are about to go through a thorough cleansing of the Self, removing all the crap of others so you can be you.

A part of being a Scorpio is being one from the past, one from another world, one who has been here and done this many times before. So, your job within this lifetime is to reveal. Your soul has been here, you have done this before. You are here to take the situations that come before you and correct them to the absolute highest. You are here to reveal the truth, and bring forth your best. Not only are you to rise up from your own ashes, so is everything that comes before you. You are an awakener; you are a revealer to what really is. Learn your power and stand in it.

Mars will be making its way into your home later this month, intensifying the energy that is already there, Neptune in Aquarius. Neptune has been moving through this area of your life for quite some time and will remain until February 2012. Neptune in Aquarius says communication in its highest, and sometimes in it's lowest. Prepare for what has been kept from you to be revealed.

May 2003

(May 2003)

SAGITTARIUS
NOV. 22 - DEC. 21

Life is all about discovering your individuality as Pluto transits your Sun sign. My suggestion to you is "Get to know Pluto." Knowing that a particular energy is present in your individuality, wouldn't you want to get to know it instead of fearing it? You know how we (human minds) are. Whatever we have a lack of knowledge about, we automatically 'hate it', 'don't like', or are afraid of it. Well, I tell you. The last thing you'll want to do fear is Pluto. Because right now, as Pluto's energy moves through your Sun sign, you will attract to you the toughest lessons possible, even your fears. Why? The planetary energy is working to bring forth your highest. Sometimes, in order to know the highest, we must live the lowest. This is just how life is. So, while you can, get to know the real energy of Pluto and allow this energy to work in its highest for you.

Even though planetary energies suggest that this is a good month for personal relationships, you may not feel the same. Saturn, which is at its very end, continues its transit through the sign of Gemini, in your room of partnership and close relationships. Saturn's energy has not been easy, nor fun, to deal with. Saturn has been directly opposing your individuality since August of 2000, telling you that everything you are, everything you do and everything you attempt to be is wrong. Oh my goodness! How did you ever survive? And to top it all off, Saturn's energy worked through those closest to you. Your mother, your brother, your sister, your best friend, your husband, your wife, and oh my goodness, even your child had an opinion or two. Well, Saturn's intent was never meant to break you down. Saturn's intent was to break down your old worn out points of view through what others reflected back to you. Anyway, Saturn's transit moves on next month. Hoorah!!! So you see, this is a good time for personal relationships. It's time for a little celebration. When you get a moment, step back and thank those lessons that were the toughest in your life.

Issues of the home / mother are one in the same. Uranus is transiting through the sign of Pisces in your room of the home / mother. Uranus breaks things down. Uranus is not a gentle approach when it needs to remove false structure. Are you living in your mother's way? Is your approach to life the same as 'your mother's?' Whatever is in your life at this time that is built on the foundation of your mother or your mother's mother, it will be broken down quickly, suddenly and unexpectedly, only so you can build it up again on your own ground.

(May 2003)

CAPRICORN
DEC. 22 - JAN. 20

Someone needs you to take care of him or her and you don't want to. The one thing you wanted the most, you now have. Yet, now that you have it, you're not sure you want it. It's all about clearing some heavy karma. You are right where you are supposed to be. The Dragon's Tail is now sweeping through the sign of Scorpio, in your eleventh room of Friends and Social. Scorpio is a karmic energy, saying that those who you attract to you throughout this lifetime are souls you have lived with before. And so, what do they want? They want you to do what you have always said you would do for them each, individually.

In this original astrology I work with, Capricorn is the decorator of the Earth. Capricorn is the energy and ability to take anything of the Earth, fix it up and make it look better. You are the energy that turned the ugly duckling into the beautiful swan. You promised a lot of little ugly ducklings that you would assist them in becoming beautiful. However, there is one in particular, and this one is actually the one you don't want to help. Yet, you must. This is your karmic deal. You must clear this up and release it once and for all. For if not, it will only come around again, and next time, harder and tougher. See the ugly duckling for what is truly is. Where is the ugly duckling in your life?

This fluctuation you are having with money is actually planetary. Neptune is moving through the sign of Aquarius right now, in your second room of Money and Material Possessions. Neptune in Aquarius says HIGH COMMUNICATION. Neptune in Aquarius says this is a time where we all are taking our talent to a much higher level. This is a time of evolution. What have you discovered your talent to be? What is your skill, your gift to the world? You are a Capricorn. You are a decorator of the Earth. What part of the world are you decorating and making beautiful? Neptune, right now, is assisting you in receiving a higher vision of your talent, so that you can manifest this upon the Earth. However, if you are just sitting around and allowing the world to serve you, then guess what? You are in for a rude awakening. Get off your tuff and do as your soul has come amongst this Earth to do. If you are poor, then you are poor in Spirit. If you are allowing your soul to do its job, you will reap the benefits of your labor. This is what Neptune in Aquarius in your second room of Material Receiving is doing. If you are allowing the mind and body to work with the soul, this will be a time of receiving greatly. However, for those of you who are not allowing your soul to do its will, then so be it, you are broke and tired.

(May 2003)

AQUARIUS
JAN. 21 - FEB. 18

You have done your service in the world, now it is time for you to do something to serve the self. You are going to a new level.

The Dragon's Tail now sweeps through the sign of Scorpio in your area of Career. Scorpio is the sign of karma, that from the past. Whatever has lain hidden in your area of career will now be revealed. Old stuff of the past will finally come up and out to the surface. Some of what is about to be revealed may make you feel as if it is time for a change, and it is. Scorpio is deep revelation. The energy holds things in for a very long time. All that has been hidden and in secret in your particular area of career will be cleansed and brought to the surface. You may find yourself suddenly out of what you are presently doing and into something totally new.

The home space consists of the Dragon's Head in the sign of Taurus. Taurus is the sign of Health, Strength and the builder. Your energies are being pulled into the home. There is something that needs to be built here. For some of you, a new home. For others of you it's time for a thorough cleansing. Perhaps it's time to tear down a wall or two. Perhaps some of you will do the wallpapering thing. Some of you may choose to paint. Whatever it is you choose to do, a restructuring will take place. And just what is the higher purpose to this restructuring of the home? The Home / Mother go hand in hand. Your foundation will change because the old ways and habits of the mother are changing.

Right now, Uranus is moving through the sign of Pisces (the home / mother) in your second room of material possessions. The message here in your second room tells me you have much stuff that either belonged to your mother, grandmother or a mother-type vibration in your life. This vibration could even be an aunt or a sister who is / was mothering to you. Anyway, personal possessions that belonged to this mother vibration will go as Uranus moves through your second room of material possessions and as the Dragon's Head transits your fourth room of Home / Mother. We are all releasing what once belonged to the mother, whether it was an old phrase she used to say or old dishes that have been passed down through the family. We are removing the old, outdated mothering habits and energies of the past for the Universe promises a new beginning.

Prepare for your home and material items to go through a deep cleansing and allow what needs to go, to go.

(May 2003)

PISCES
FEB. 19 - MAR. 19

Even though this is a very good month to do a little extra work around the home, you may feel more of an urge to create. Many of you Pisces individuals will discover a new talent, or enhance an already existing one.

The message I get for you, is to begin in the home. Clean out your space. This is a good time of year for you to fine-tune your energy and space in the home. Go through your closets, drawers and so on. Go through boxes that have been lying around for quite some time. Spirit gives me a vision that this cleansing will better take place between you and another. Allow one close to you to assist you in this desirable chore of cleaning. Really, this can be fun.

After cleaning the home and creating space for energy to flow, an incredible blast of creativity will begin to flow through you. There is a full moon total eclipse in the sign of Scorpio this month, which will take place in your ninth room of Higher Knowledge and your third room of Communication. Again, a new talent exposes itself, or one that you are already working on will enhance greatly.

Scorpio is the sign of karma, from the past. This burst of knowledge that you are about to experience is something your soul has brought with it. So therefore, it's not really something new. It may feel new to the mind, however, it is something that is already contained within you, and this is the time for it to expose itself. The energy of this gift feels absolutely incredible. You are about to experience a power you have only imagined. You see? The old saying goes, "If you can imagine it, you can become it." This is so true. For our imagination truly is the monitor of the soul. Believe me, if you can visualize it in your head, it has already happened, and perhaps you have returned to take whatever this vision is to the next level. Whatever you do, put forth your best and do the best you absolutely can do.

Your health and physical strength are phenomenal due to Jupiter, planet of abundance, moving through your sixth room of Health and the Physical Body. You will want to take it slow when eating, for not only will Jupiter increase your energy, it will greatly increase your appetite, which in turn may greatly increase your physical size. Now, for those of you who want to attract additional weight gain, and then by all means, go for it.

(May 2003)

ARIES
MAR. 20 - APR. 19

A beautiful Full Moon Total Eclipse, in the sign of Scorpio, will be taking place this month in your eighth room of Partner's Resources and in the your second room of Money and Material Possessions. The first thing I want to advice you to do is make room. Aries people hold to on to quite a bit of stuff. This great eclipse promises new things to come into your life through another. However, you must first make room in your life for these new things to come in. If your life is already full and complete, these destined gifts of the soul will have a new place in your life. Whether you think you need / want these things or not, they are destined to come in, and the only way these things can come into your life is if there is a place for them. Use this time to do a little clearing and prepare for these gifts of the soul to be brought into your life. Spirits says to recognize that what you receive at this time is reward from the Universe for work you have done in the past.

Uranus has moved into your twelfth room of Karma and Spirituality. Uranus is the planet of sudden activity. It is like lightening; you never know when or where it is going to strike. Moments of the past will come around suddenly and unexpectedly; things that are buried within will be exposed to your physical world. Do you have any long time secrets that you have keep buried within? Guess what, when you least expect it, those secrets will be revealed. Uranus is actually taking you through a cleansing of the soul, uncovering all that is hidden so that you can deal with these things, once and for all. Don't try to fight it. Just allow your soul to be cleansed so that you can move on freely and happily. Uranus will go retrograde next month, relaxing its energies, giving you the opportunity to do this cleansing of the soul all of your own. However, if you choose not to, Uranus will return direct again in November, resuming its mission. You can either do it yourself, or let Uranus do it for you.

Jupiter is moving into a direct opposition with Neptune, and Mars will be crossing Neptune. Again, childhood secrets will be revealed. Whatever took place in your life when you were a child will come up and out into the open through the younger ones around you. This is a time of cleansing the soul. Just go with the flow of energy that is presented to you and clean your spiritual closet. Remember, there is a great reward that is headed your way, a reward of the soul, one that is destined to be yours. However, this all depends on how well you have cleaned your closets, your physical and spiritual ones.

(May 2003)

TAURUS
APR. 20 - MAY 20

Planetary activity is lining up heavily around you, as in the Self. You are really trying to figure life out, aren't you? Well, as the Dragon's Tail sweeps through the sign of Scorpio, in your seventh room of partnership and close relationships, this is really of time of detaching from the business of others and getting to know the self.

Who are you? Why are you here? What is your purpose in this world? This is what this time is all about for you. For those of you who are in a relationship, take a deep breath and step aside for a while. This is a time for you to find YOU, and right now, planetary energies are on your side to make this very possible.

Mercury moved into retrograde position April 26 in your Sun sign of Taurus. Mercury is the planet of communication and expression. Mercury, I am sure, has been wreaking havoc on the way you present yourself to others. Perhaps you will really want to take your time when communicating with others; your thoughts will confuse whatever it is you are trying to say. Mercury retrograde in your first room of Self says move slowly and take your time when getting dressed in the mornings. For what you wear will have all to do with how you express yourself to others. Our outer appearance says a lot, and right now, as Mercury moves retrograde in your first room of Self, what you say may not come out the way you really mean. Just remember to slow down and take it easy when communicating with others at this time. Mercury returns direct on the 20th of this month.

Beautiful Venus will be moving into your Sun sign of Taurus this month, absolutely enhancing everything about you. After Mercury returns direct on the 20th, lovely Venus will be right by it's side, absolutely illuminating you. So you see, all you have to do is wait for the time to be right to express yourself in your highest.

A beautiful Full Moon Total Eclipse will be taking place this month in the sign of Scorpio, which places this energy in your seventh room of Partnership and Close Relationships. An incredibly dramatic change will take place in this particular area of your life. What is it you want? You must first figure out the answer to this question before you proceed with the relationship you are in. Are you wanting and willing to walk these next two years alone, or are you willing to work with the differences you have to deal with in your relationship? Figure out what it is you really want, for this eclipse will seal in your choice.

(May 2003)

GEMINI
MAY 21 - JUN. 20

You are in preparation for a new year of your life to begin. Do you know what you want? Do you know where you want to go, be and do for the next year? Right now, planetary energies are lining up heavily above you, in the area of visions. Within your visions are messages to the mind from the soul. These messages are communicating with you about what your soul desires to do and where it desires to be. It is up to you to listen to your soul. It is up to you to figure out how to align with what your soul has come amongst the Earth to do.

A very powerful Full Moon Total Eclipse will take place this month, in the sign of Scorpio, placing this energy in your room of Health and the Physical Body. Depending upon where you are at this particular moment in your life has all to do with how this eclipse will affect you.

The Dragon's Tail is also sweeping through your sixth room of Health and the Physical Body, actually performing a cleansing in this area. Your physical body is going through a cleansing so that your spiritual body has a stronger place to dwell. And because the Dragon's Tail is sweeping through the sign of Scorpio, old issues of the past will resurface. If there are any unresolved issues that lay within the physical body at this time, the Dragon's Tail will sweep through them and cause them to come up to the surface, just so you can face them and clear them, once and for all. The Dragon's Tail will be moving through this area of your life until December 2004. You have from now until then to heal your physical self.

Uranus has moved into your tenth room of Career, bringing forth energy of sudden change. Your career is about to go through a sudden and possibly unforeseen change. Is this a positive change? Of course it is. All change is positive, whether you see it this way or not. This change in the area of Career looks to involve a move or relocation. This looks to be exactly what your soul needs at this time. Prepare for a very positive change to take place in your area of career.

Your life is about to take a sudden twist and turn due to planetary energies working to place you in alignment with the will of your soul. And, just what exactly is that? You are about to find out. Perhaps, planetary energies want to move you from one state to another, in an attempt to align you with soul mate, considering Pluto is moving retrograde in your seventh room of Partnership. Some of you are already connected to your soul, yet are you aligned? We will soon see.

(May 2003)

Planetary energies show that you have been thinking a lot about moving, changing residence or relocating. Planets are lining up way outside of the home area, making you want to be "there" also.

A new life awaits you. Uranus, planet of sudden change, is moving through your area of travel. Uranus is the power to make things happen suddenly and unexpectedly. Uranus will transit through this area of your life until March 2011, during which time, you will find yourself moving around a lot, going from one to the next, picking up one form of study then going to something totally different. Uranus is change, and brings about difference. So during this time of Uranus transiting your ninth room, don't be surprised if you find yourself living in other countries or places that are foreign to you.

This month also brings about a Full Moon Total Eclipse in your fifth room of children, opposing your eleventh room of friends, bringing about new people in your life, possibly those of other cultures and races. This is absolutely fantastic, considering the Uranus energy moving through your ninth room. You may even find yourself wanting to study a new civilization.

Some of you will find yourself unexpectedly pregnant during this time, and considering how the planets are moving around in your life, this is unadvisable. Planetary energies suggest great complications and possibly even miscarriage. Use better judgment.

Saturn entered into the sign of Gemini in August of 2000, bringing together soul mates of al kinds. However, these soul mates that came together had a great amount of karma to clear, and many relationships did not make it through the challenge of clearing. Saturn moving through Gemini has no been easy for anyone. For you, this Saturn in Gemini has been moving through your twelfth room of karma. DOUBLE WHAMMY! Yes, that's right. Many of you ended old relationships and began new ones with a lover from the past. Many of you had a very difficult time dealing with the differences that existed between the two of you, so therefore parted ways. Well, Saturn does move on, out of the sign of Gemini, yet into your Sun sign, next month, and will be in the in the sign of Cancer until July 2005. Saturn moving through your first room of Self, will magnify the worst, only so you can make it better. This is a time of intense improvement of the Self.

(May 2003)

LEO
JUL. 23 - AUG. 22

It is all about Career, socializing, friends and other people. Your energies are radiating positive vibrations. This months Full Moon will be a Total Eclipse in Scorpio, placing this energy in your Home and Career. It is all about Career. The Dragon's Tail is sweeping through your home at this time, possibly bringing forth an intense cleansing, and for many of you, a complete change in residence. The Dragon's Tail is sweeping through the sign of Scorpio, karma and stuff from the past. This is a time of going through everything in your home and clearing the past once and for all. Things you have been holding on to for way too long must go. Your energies are being pulled into the outer world, into career.

Mars will cross over Neptune this month in the sign of Aquarius, in your seventh room of Partnership and close relationships, possibly stirring things up a bit. Neptune is at a stand still (stationary) going retrograde (backward) for the next five months. And, just what does this mean for relationships for you? Well, it really isn't all that good, that is, if you're trying to hold on to something that just is not there. A pull away will occur. Uranus, moving through the sign of Pisces, in your eighth room of Partner's Resources, is also stationary this month, and will go retrograde at the beginning of next month. Jupiter, planet of abundance, is moving through your first room of Self right now, in the sign of Leo, blessing you with an incredible power, motivation and leadership to walk your path as a single. However, it does not mean you will be single forever. Just at this time.

This is a time for you to re-identify with yourself. Jupiter transiting through your Sun sign says power. The Dragon's Head, Mercury and Venus are all moving through your tenth room of Career this month, as the upcoming new moon and Saturn move through your eleventh room of Friends and Social. It is all about Career. It is all about you finding and connecting with your real power, alone.

Planetary energies are pulling those whom you think you need by your side away. A space is being cleared, for it is time for you as an individual to find yourself and do what your soul has come to the Earth to do. Your true power and oneness that exists within you is coming out. It is time for you to learn to stand on your own two feet. If you are allowing yourself to not "hang on" to whatever needs to go, you will do absolutely fine. Let whatever needs to go, go. Connect and Be ONE with your power.

(May 2003)

VIRGO
AUG. 23 - SEPT. 22

A great idea happens this month, one concerning career, something that you and another can do together.

Saturn, planet of karma and tough challenges, has been moving through your career since August of 2000. Saturn says there have been many things to clear in this area of your life, things that began a long time ago. Saturn moved through this area of your life, activating and bringing forth any and all that existed here and needed to be cleared. Most was not easy to deal with, however, Saturn will be moving on next month. Yet, before Saturn is totally done with this area, it will leave one last gift, a person.

You are about to connect with someone who will need your assistance. There are those who have assisted you and helped you along the way, and now, you are attracting to you someone who needs your help. This task is a part of your karma. You are born with great intelligence and foresight. Virgo's are blessed with the ability to see things from a different level. This is what makes most of you strong leaders. Saturn says that before it is finished in your life, it is dropping off a person, a karmic one, one whom your soul is destined to assist. If you allow yourself to do as your soul is destined to do, in the next two years, you will receive an incredible monetary reward. This will be the Universe's way of rewarding you for doing what your soul has come to do.

A change in residence may also be taking place this month, due to a sudden change in a relationship. Uranus, planet of sudden change, is now moving through your seventh room of partnership and close relationships. Uranus is stationary (at a stand still) right now, preparing to go retrograde (backward) next month. This signifies an ending to a close relationship. However, while Uranus is still direct, someone will suddenly come into your life, and then will suddenly leave. Yet, this particular someone will return sometime in November.

For those of you who are in a particular relationship right now, a sudden change will present itself. Is it meant for you and this person to be together and stay together forever? We'll see. Uranus moving through your seventh room of Partnership and close relationships says sudden changes are about to take place. An old relationship will end, and a new one will begin. This new relationship that is about to start is indeed the person you are destined to assist.

(May 2003)

LIBRA
SEP. 23 - OCT. 22

Last year, as the Dragon's Head heavily moved through the sign of Gemini in your ninth room of Higher Knowledge, Education and Travel. A soul mate / soul partner was brought to you, one who brought about many opportunities to travel and learn. This person also brought about an opportunity for you to change careers. Did you? This month brings a Full Moon Total Eclipse in the sign of Scorpio, placing this energy in your second room of Money and Material Possessions. Your life is about to totally change, at least in the area of how you make your money. An opportunity of the past presents itself. Last years energies brought forth an opportunity, through someone else, for you to change what you were currently doing, as far as career. If you accepted the opportunity, your life is about to take off if a very positive direction. If you did not, you will find yourself in the total opposite of where you 'could' be.

Even though family members may be very needing of you at this time, your higher energies are being pulled outside of the home, with the people. Jupiter, planet of abundance, is moving through your eleventh room of Friends and Social, enhancing the number of people you meet through your many travels. That's right, you will be finding yourself going to many places you have not been before, all for the sake of enhancing your social skills and allowing your soul to come forth and be who it is within this world. And, there is someone by your side, willing to assist you every step of the way.

Libra, you are the sign that represents social, friends and entertainment. You are the gatherer of many people. What are you gathering the people for? Why, all of a sudden, are many people coming around you and giving you their attention? There is a higher order to all of this. There is 'something' that you and another have worked on together to present to the world. Presentation begins.

As the Dragon's Tail sweeps through your second room of material possessions, a time of intense cleansing is upon you. This is a time for you to release personal possessions of the past. It is time to let go and move on. If you are allowing yourself to move in alignment with your Divine path, there will be someone close by to assist you with every step you take, even if it is something you call 'yours.' Libras have a way of always caring for another. Now, this is your time to be cared for. Realize that this is a reflection of what you have done before. We reap what we sow.

(May 2003)

SCORPIO
OCT. 23 - NOV. 21

The Dragon's Tail now sweeps through your Sun sign, being activated by a Full Moon Total Eclipse, in Scorpio, this month. It's about marriage. It's about solidifying a relationship / partnership. It's about accepting assistance from another. It's about your home, your career, your money, everything! This Full Moon Total Eclipse is taking place in your first room of Self. Everything about your Self is about to change dramatically.

Leo is the sign that rules your place / standing within the world, and at this time, Jupiter, planet of abundance, is transiting this area. Jupiter brings forth monetary and material enhancement, and because it is traveling through the sign of Leo, the energy will bring forth power. Much of this power you are about to experience is due to the alignment of you and another person who stepped into your life sometime ago. This person whom you attracted in your life, within the last two years, has a lot to do with this awakening that is occurring in your life. This is a dramatic time for you, a time of giving up the Self, trusting and relying on someone else.

Mars will cross Neptune this month, in your area of the home, causing things that have been hidden and kept from you to come out in the open and reveal it self. These secrets look to have something to do with your family members.

Mercury returns direct this month as Venus walks by its side. If you have had suspicion of the partner, well. There are definitely things going on around you that are not in the up and up. As the Dragon's Tail sweeps through the sign of Scorpio, in your first room of Self, many things of past will come up and out and reveal itself to you. The truth will be known. The Dragon's Tail is representing the past. The old 'you' will come out and express themselves through others. What goes around comes around.

Planetary energies do suggest that someone is nearby who will want to assist something you do. Yet, Saturn is near by and will present issues of trust. Make sure that if you do sign on with anyone, you thoroughly understand all papers that will need to be signed. Leave no 'letter' left understood. This opportunity can prove to be a good one, yet you must make sure you have a complete understanding of all that is going on. And, because Scorpio is such an intuitive sign, make sure you use your intuition in all you do. Never doubt yourself.

June 2003

(June 2003)

SAGITTARIUS
NOV. 22 - DEC. 21

In August of 2000, Saturn moved into the sign of Gemini, placing its energy in your seventh room of partnerships and close relationships. Saturn wreaked havoc of relationships of all kinds, especially with you. Saturn came into your life and actually turned it upside down and inside out, causing you to take a very close look at whom you are. Who are you and why are you here, were questions, I am sure, many of you asked during this Saturn transit. Saturn is the Lord of Karma, bringing back around old relationship issues from the past and also from previous lifetimes. Many souls who came together under the Saturn in Gemini transit are old karmic soul mates who came together to clear old karma, so that they can move on through life as a higher individual. Some will choose to stay together, yet many will split apart.

Many of you Sag's will come to a decision to either stay with the one you are with, or to move on. Considering the way the planets have lined up for you this month, I say most of you will continue on with the one you are with. Planetary energies are making it a little easier for you, personally, to deal with the differences that were magnified in the last two years. Hopefully, you have learned the value of judgment and no longer allow yourself to viciously judge another. Hopefully, you have learned much about yourself from what you attracted to you through others.

Anyway, Saturn has moved on, out of the sign of Gemini, out of your room of Partnership, yet now, into the sign of Cancer, and into your room of Sex, Debts and the Partner's Resources. Yes, the partner you are with now will want to assist you financially, yet, this person will want to see you bringing in a significant amount of money also. Do not allow yourself to fall into a state of dependency. Saturn will not put up with it, and you won't like the way it tells you so.

Mars will cross over Uranus this month in your area of the Home, creating some old energy to stir up there. Get rid of the "mother's junk." Stop holding on to what belonged to the mother, grandmother and so forth. It is time you clear your life of the mother's habits, issues, and ways and, most of all material stuff. It is time for you to learn to stand as the Sagittarius individual that you are and give yourself a personality.

(June 2003)

CAPRICORN
DEC. 22 - JAN. 20

Saturn has now moved into your area of partnership and close relationships. All of a sudden, the one you wanted desperately to be with will suddenly be an instant turn off. Saturn in the area of partnership is not an easy transit to deal with. Saturn brings forth old stuff, old karma and un-dealt with issues pertaining to old relationships. Saturn is about to test you to the core. All you can do for the next two years, as Saturn transits this area of your life, is do the best you can do. I tell you, Saturn transiting the room of partnership has to be the most difficult of all, for Saturn is directly opposing your Sun sign, which means the energy is directly opposing you. You will, at many times, feel you are dating the Devil himself, and you are. For many of you Capricorn individuals, this test of Saturn will present itself to you through your children, family members and love relationship. Old crap from the past is about to resurface yet, it doesn't mean run, hide and get away from it. It means face these challenges, once and for all, and get on with your life. Clear this karmic energy and allow yourself to live.

Mars will cross over Uranus this month in your area of Communication and Expression, making you say or do something that is totally not in the highest. BE PATIENT with whomever you are dealing with. Mars crossing Uranus will make you act suddenly, abruptly and impulsively. You may find yourself saying and / or doing something you will later regret. Do not let these energies control you. Keep yourself in control. A very positive way of using this Mars / Uranus conjunction is to write. Express these intense emotions on paper and release them that way.

Some of you will attract a new love into your life, for Venus is on her way to your room of partnership and close relationships. Many of you will want absolutely nothing to do with a love relationship at this time because of Saturn's transit here. Saturn has the tendency to make us want to be alone rather than to deal with the challenges of others. Yet, you know? We are all here to learn and grow, and by pushing away what appears to be tough, unbearable or undesirable, we limit ourselves. We keep the self from learning and growing. Well, it is totally up to you whether or not you allow someone to be in your life at this time or not. Realize that what you are going through in the area of personal relationships is indeed a karmic experience. Do your best to deal with it and clear it. Planetary energies are standing by with a great reward.

(June 2003)

AQUARIUS
JAN. 21 - FEB. 18

Many of you Aquarians have either met someone new, or enhanced the already existing love relationship you are in. Jupiter, planet of abundance, is moving direct through your room of partnership, enhancing personal relationships of all kinds in your life. Jupiter transiting through your room of partnership brings forth marriage. Its abundant energy solidifies and enhances. Congratulations to all of you, who are walking in alignment with this energy, and I hope to be invited to your wedding.

Saturn moves into your room of Health for the next two years, bringing forth any and all health related issues that you may not have thoroughly dealt with in the past. Saturn is the Lord of Karma and wherever it transits in our life, it brings forth un-dealt with issues of the past, just so we can deal with them, once and for all, clear them, and move on. Saturn says, that while its energy is transiting this area of your life, old stuff from the past will be ignited and brought to the forefront. These could even be old un-dealt with issues of previous lifetimes. Because Saturn is transiting through the sign of Cancer, these issues will have to do with Sex and old debts. If there are old unpaid debts that need to be faced, know they will be faced through Saturn passing through this area of your life. If there are old un-dealt with issues related to sex, they will be brought forth, and from this you may need to seek some sort of counseling to assist you in dealing with these old issues. And, you will want to deal with them and clear them, for if you do not, the longer they sit, the worse they will become. And remember, this energy is taking place in your area of health. Saturn will transit this area of your life until July of 2005.

Mars will cross Uranus in your area of money and material possessions. Yes, for you too, it is time to clean out your closets. Uranus is moving through the sign of Pisces, which rules the energy of the mother. Uranus goes retrograde this month, asking you to please use this time to clean your closets of the mother's stuff. Mars crossing Uranus will intensify this energy a thousand times or more. This is definitely a time of releasing yourself from the energy of your own mother, and your own mothering ways. The Dragon's Head is moving through the sign of Taurus in your room of the Home / Mother, connecting with the energies of Uranus and Mars moving through the sign of Pisces. The message is, release yourself from the old ways of the mother and allow yourself to connect with your higher side.

(June 2003)

PISCES
FEB. 19 - MAR. 19

Saturn finally moves out of your home and into your room of children. Saturn is the Lord of Karma, bringing forth old un-dealt with issues of the past. Whatever old un-dealt with issues you have lying within this area of your life, they will be ignited and brought forth for you to face and clear, once and for all. For you, this Saturn energy is in your area of the children and siblings. Old childhood issues related to your own children, issues related to those whom you grew up with will all of a sudden will be remembered. Some, you may not be prepared to face, however, all you must. This is a time of clearing this old energy out of this area. This is a time of releasing yourself from the past, so you can move on in the now.

Issues of children will come up strongly this month, some of you trying to decide whether or not timing is appropriate to begin a family. Some of you will give birth to your babies at this time, finding that the soul you have just given physical life to be one who will be very difficult to control. That's because it is not meant for us to control anyone. Bringing a soul into the world during this time of Saturn transiting this area of your life says you will birth a complete reflection of your soul. Everything you have been and everything your soul has experienced will be reflected to you through this child. For those of you who are not having children at this time, this reflection will come to you through other people's children and through your family members. This is just that time within your life where Saturn's job is to give you a complete reflection of yourself through your children, other people's children and / or your family members. Much of this will be difficult to handle because of Saturn's directness and intensity. Just do your best to recognize the reflection.

Uranus is now transiting through your first room of Self, for the next 7 years. This month, Uranus will go retrograde. After Uranus goes retrograde, Mars will transit across it. No, you are not having a nervous breakdown, well, some of you might. Anyway, Mars crossing Uranus in your Sun sign says a cleansing of the outer personality, suddenly quickly and unexpectedly. This planetary alignment will bring forth nervous activity and feelings of shakiness. That's because old energies and habits are being shaken off of you. Relaxation, meditation and massage are great modalities to assist you in getting through this time.

(June 2003)

ARIES
MAR. 20 - APR. 19

Karma is about to hit you in many different areas of your life.

First of all, Uranus is now transiting through the sign of Pisces, in your twelfth room of karma. Uranus will bring forth old issues of the mother, your own mothering issues, and any and all previous lifetime karmic experiences that lie within your karmic closet. Memories of the past will be ignited and will come up strongly. Early this month, Uranus will go retrograde in this area of karma, and then Mars will stroll along and cross it, intensifying its energy and causing your thoughts to go haywire. You will find yourself seeing things in your head, and will have absolutely no idea why these visions are coming in the way they are. Old stuff from previous lifetimes is being ignited. You are going through a remembering of the things you once went through, and most of these memories will have to do you with the home, children and sex. This is a time of prayer and cleansing. Allow you to be cleansed and released from this past lifetime experience.

Many Aries adults are about to find themselves repeating an experience from a previous lifetime or when you were a child. Spirit says memories of the home when growing up will come forth. This is a time of releasing the past, as it is for all of us. We are going back home. We are going back to a time that made us into the persons we are this day. However, Spirit says, this person whom we are right now is to enhance and change. Many of us will not want to change. Many of you will think you cannot. Well, for those of you who are afraid to get help and clear yourself from the past that haunts you, and then so be it. Shall you dwell in your mess? Many of you will get the help you will need to assist you in releasing the past. And so be it to you, also. May you walk and dwell in the highest of your spiritual order.

Some of you Aries individuals will bare children at this time, as Jupiter, planet of abundance, moves through your fifth room of children. Some of you will pull other peoples children to you. You will receive a multitude of messages to you through the children.

Saturn moves into your home this month, transiting through the sign of Cancer. Cancer, in the original astrology is the sign that rules Sex and Debts. This month marks the beginning of old karmic issues related to the mother, the home, your childhood, children around you, old karmic debts, and inappropriate sexual behavior. Use this time to clear this old energy, so that you may walk in your highest order.

(June 2003)

TAURUS
APR. 20 - MAY 20

Saturn officially moves out of your second room of money and material receiving, early this month, clearing the energy there, allowing you the opportunity, to once again, attract money to yourself. Actually, Saturn in Gemini, for you, was in a very positive space. Saturn in Gemini was attempting to connect you with one who shares the same vision / dream as you. You and another were destined to come together during Saturn in Gemini to manifest your dream. Did you do it? Did you allow yourself to connect with one who shared the same vision as you?

The Dragon's Tail is now sweeping through the sign of Scorpio (karma) in your room of partnership and close relationships. This planetary aspect signifies a cleansing being performed in this area of your life. Old secrets and issues that have been kept inside will suddenly be released through this sweeping of the Dragon's Tail. Old relationships will come around once again for the sake of being cleared, released and taken to a higher level. The Dragon's Head moving through your first room of Self in the sign of Taurus, indicates a healing of the personality, outer appearance and character. As the Dragon's Head moves through your Sun sign, a strengthening of the personality will occur. Many of you who walk in alignment with the will of your soul will be absolutely amazed of the beauty that is about to present itself through you.

This is also a time for Taurus people to connect with their oneness. Planetary energies are also lining up in the area of communication, presenting a time of manifesting a plan your soul has come upon the Earth to carry out. Be still and quiet your mind. Your spirit within wants to communicate with you. Write down everything you see in what you may call, your imagination. For truly the imagination is the soul communicating with the mind. Closely pay attention to your dreams, visions and ideas that suddenly come about, for within these are the plan of your soul.

Jupiter's energy is enhancing your home at this time, possibly wanting to do a little extra cleansing or change the furniture around. There are also a few new things you may attract to you, also, things to decorate the home. Some of you will attract a new home through the energy of Jupiter here. Yet, for each one of you, Jupiter will bring forth an abundance of change, growth and expansion.

(June 2003)

GEMINI
MAY 21 - JUN. 20

Saturn officially moves out of your Sun sign early this month, creating an opening for that new you to expose itself to the world. As Saturn (Lord of Karma) moved through your first room of Self in the last two and a half years, I know you went through some pretty intense bouts with your identity. One moment your masculine side would come through and the next your feminine. You just could not decide who you wanted to be: The responsible one or the weak one, the child or the adult. Well now Saturn moves out of your Sun sign and into the sign of Cancer, placing its energy in your second room of material possessions.

Saturn has now placed its energy in your second room of money and material possessions, transiting through the sign of Cancer until July of 2005. Saturn transiting through this area of your life will bring about a sort of stinginess where 'me' and 'mine' are considered. You will receive a gift through one younger than yourself, where you may find yourself in a total lack of appreciation. Watch what you say and how you say it, for things have a way of coming back around. Yet, before they do, they have a way of swelling and growing and becoming more intense, and then when the time comes, they come back around, staring you in the face and saying "Remember me?" So before you react to receiving this gift you may not want to receive, just remember karma. Then again, what you receive for this birthday will be very symbolic of what you gave to another.

For the last year and a half, the Dragon's Tail has swept through your room of Partnership and close relationships. There were times, I am sure, where you felt as though you could not stay in your relationship for another minute. Yet, some of you stayed, and others of you left. Well, now that Saturn (Lord of Karma) has entered into your room of receiving, all that you have dished out to another will come around and be dished out to you. Also, the Dragon's Tail is now sweeping through your room of Health, in the sign of Scorpio. More karma.

Were you helpful to others when you were needed, or did you half-do, or maybe not do at all? Guess what Gemini. This energy is all coming back around. Whatever you have put out to others will come back around at this time. Allow yourself to see the reflection in these situations and then clear them as best you can. Put forth your best, put out your best, always do your best, for things do always return.

(June 2003)

Planetary energies are all wanting to take you outside of the home and into the outer world, where you think you belong. Perhaps you do, at this time.

The Dragon's Tail is now sweeping through your area of the children and family members. Are you 'giving up' for a while? Sure looks like it. The Dragon's Tail is sweeping through Scorpio, the sign of karma, clearing out the old karmic energy you may have there. For some of you who have younger children, you may find yourself doing something to promote a child who has demonstrated a particular talent, something that reminds you of yourself when you were younger.

Saturn will move into the sign of Cancer this month, placing this energy in your Sun sign. Saturn is the Lord of Karma. Saturn moving through this area of your life will bring forth identities from lifetimes ago. You are about to find yourself wearing many different hats, skirts, pants and shoes. A multitude of personalities are about to come forth through this power of Saturn moving through your Sun sign. And just what is this all about? This is about remembering and clearing the many different lifetimes you have lived. As your outer identity changes, a different lifetime presents itself. Yeah, you may feel like you have multiple personality disorder. You will be exposing multiple personalities; yet, the only way this can become a disorder is when you choose not to deal with them. Face these many lifetimes you have lived, and free your soul into being whom it truly is this day.

Uranus and Mars are moving through your room of Higher Knowledge and Travel. Both energies indicate sudden movement. Uranus will make things happen suddenly, quickly and unexpectedly, and Mars brings on the aggression. Pay extra close attention while driving. These two planetary energies will make you want to speed and drive somewhat erratically. Remain focused when driving, or you might not want to drive at all.

Cancer, your life is really about to change. Planetary energies are bringing forth an opportunity for you to be out in the world with many people, learning many new things. This is a chance for you to experience life in its fullest. However, you must remain in control of everything you do. If you are careless with your life, these energies will turn the other way. Have the greatest respect for you.

(June 2003)

LEO
JUL. 23 - AUG. 22

Saturn moves into the sign of Cancer this month, placing this energy in your room of karma, above your sun. Saturn is about to twist and distort your thoughts and visions. Saturn is awakening the karma that lay within this area of your life. Pay attention to your dreams and to the visions you receive, for these are messages from your soul, letting you know places you have been and things you have done. Many of these visions you receive will not be well accepted by your mind, and many you will have great difficulty with. Yet know that as these visions come forth, they will need to be recognized and cleared. Saturn moving through your room of karma is awakening your past for the sake of clearing. Do the best you can do to clear this energy.

Jupiter continues to move through your first room of Self, blessing you with this awesome power to advance in your individuality. During this time, a magnificent you will expose itself. Now that Saturn has moved into your room of karma, an incredible amount of karmic debt is about to expose itself. As these things of the past resurface, clear them one at a time. This clearing will allow Jupiter's energy to do a better job at revealing your true power.

Old issues related to the mother and the home you grew up in will ignite and expose itself to you this month. Once again, do your best to clear these emotional issues of the past. Planetary energies are moving through each water sign in our astrological system, activating old emotional stuff that may be tied, connected and / or related to the mother. If you feel you need assistance in clearing these feelings, then by all means, get it. This is a pretty intense time for everyone, having to deal with emotional issues of the past. You are not the only one. The last you will want to do is shut down and not talk about it at all. This will only hold the energy inside, which may later cause you to get ill, or release this energy in a very harmful way to others. Take a deep breath and allow the mind and soul to cleanse itself of these intense emotional energies of the past.

A good place to focus your energies is in the area of career. The Dragon's Head (success) is moving through this area of your life until late December 2004. Something you have wanted to do for a very long time will expose itself through the transit of the Dragon's Head. You will also receive a vision of how this is to take place. Do your best to keep your mind open to receive these messages from your soul.

(June 2003)

VIRGO
AUG. 23 - SEPT. 22

Everyone seems to be going through a bit of karma these days. For you Virgo, Jupiter, planet of abundance, is moving through your room karma from now until August, bringing back around an abundance of events that took place concerning your friends. As I look into your room of friends, I see Saturn moving into this area for the next two years. Saturn (Lord of Karma) in this area doesn't look too pleasant. Saturn looks a little annoyed. Considering all of the karmic energy that is taking place in your life, it looks like much of your karma will have to do with your friends at this time. All you can do is face / clear them in the absolute highest. Try not to let these issues get you down.

Uranus (sudden change) moves into retrograde position this month your area of partnership. Uranus has a way of making things happen suddenly and unexpectedly. With Uranus going retrograde, a close relationship you are in may suddenly end. Shortly after Uranus goes retrograde, Mars (aggression) will cross over Uranus, intensifying what takes place. There is a particular relationship whose time has just come to its end. Perhaps all that needed to take place has taken place and now you are free to move on in another direction. Spirit asks that you examine why this relationship went the way it did. This relationship that ends under this transit was with a person who just did not fit the bill. This person was indeed a square trying to fit into the space of a circle. Realize this and let it go. Remember you are going through a time of karmic clearing with relationships.

This is a time of concentrating your energies on your career. Forget about relationships for a while and allow your thoughts to focus on your place within this world. Venus will be entering into the sign of Gemini on the 10th of this month, assisting you and another to come together and work on some sort of plan. Whatever this plan is, it involves something you can do to help and assist many people. Pay attention to the fine details and allow yourself to move slowly through this venture. If you allow your mind to listen to the suggestion of the other person, all should go rather well. However, if you decide not to listen, you will only cause friction between yourself and the other, and at this point in time, that is the last thing you will want to do. Planetary energies lining up in your eleventh room of other people suggest that there are others who might want to involve themselves in this plan. Just pay attention to how you feel about their presence. Use your highest judgment.

(June 2003)

LIBRA
SEP. 23 - OCT. 22

Saturn moves into the sign of Cancer this month, placing its energy in your tenth room of career. Are you doing what your soul has really come here to do, or are you in a career mainly for cash? Saturn in this area will test what you are presently doing, making sure it is what you are here to do and not something you are just doing. However, Saturn is also the Lord of Karma. A situation from the past comes back around. Are you capable of doing what is being presented to you to do? This work involves socializing with many people, and sometimes one-on-one. There is a great amount of money to be made doing this job, however, remember this is something that is coming in to you through the energy of Saturn. Now, don't get me wrong. Saturn is not a 'bad' energy. Saturn is the test of the self to see how far a person will allow himself / herself to go for money, in this case. You know the old saying, "selling your soul to the devil?" Have you ever thought about what this really means? Why don't you think about it, now?

You might want to think at least ten times before accepting anything. Uranus (planet of sudden change) will turn retrograde this month in your room of health. Shortly after Uranus goes retrograde, Mars (planet of physical aggression) will transit across Uranus, intensifying its energy. Whatever has lain hidden within the physical body will come up and out at this time, and Mars energy will intensify it. Use extreme precautions, especially during intimate moments, for this planetary energy is taking place in an emotional sign.

The Dragon's Tail is sweeping through the sign of Scorpio, in your room of money and material gain. The way you have made your money looks like it is about to change. A proposition comes forth this month, one that looks to have been offered months ago. What will you do? First you must lose the judgment of the situation and allow yourself to see above and beyond the physical. An opportunity to make a sufficient amount of money has approached you, however, you look as if your own personal judgments may cause you to walk away. It is our judgment that keeps us from succeeding. We have given ourselves so many reasons to say 'No' that it keeps us from experiencing life in its fullest, so therefore, we continue to walk around 'wanting.' Uranus moving through the sign of Pisces represents how the mother's ways are being looked at, examined and let go of. Times are changing. There is a God light that exists in each and every situation that presents itself upon this earth. Find the light in yours.

(June 2003)

SCORPIO
OCT. 23 - NOV. 21

Saturn moves into the sign of Cancer this month, placing its energy in your room of Higher Knowledge and Travel. No matter how sweet someone may make something seem to be, remember who you are and use your better judgment. Planetary energies are lining up in such a way where someone may use certain tactics to lure you into their plan. Use precaution. Yet more so than that, use your intuition.

Jupiter, planet of abundance, continues its transit through the sign of Leo in your room of career, bringing forth energy of enhancement. Leo represents Higher Knowledge and Travel. Don't be surprised if you find yourself traveling for business. You now have the opportunity to stand out more than ever. Jupiter is abundance and power, especially when placed in the room of career. Know what you are stepping into and use this power and energy of Jupiter in its absolute highest. A time of recognition is upon you. Use this energy well.

The Dragon's Head has moved into your room of partnership, bringing forth to those of you who want it, a partner who assists. Are you looking for an assistant? Are you looking for a promoter? Are you looking for someone you can assist and promote? Whatever the case may be, this person is here. Just remember to use your higher intelligence when making any and all decisions. Someone has a very tricky tongue and will try desperately hard to use it on you.

Uranus will move into a retrograde position this month, placing this energy in your fifth room of children. Shortly thereafter, Mars will pass over retrograde Uranus, intensifying its energy. This energy will have to do with a family member. Watch closely your little ones around the water.

The Dragon's Tail continues to sweep through your first room of Self, eliminating one thing after the other from your life. You are going through a deep cleansing. Some of you may experience the loss of someone close to you. Do not try to hold on to anything at this time, and allow yourself to receive the higher meaning. Your higher Self is preparing to expose itself to the world, and in order for this to happen, a cleansing of the Self must take place. As you feel the need to do so, clean out your closets and eliminate. Once again, do not try to hold on to anything at this time. Just remember to allow yourself to connect with your highest spiritual guides and receive the highest message there is.

July 2003

(July 2003)

SAGITTARIUS
NOV. 22 - DEC. 21

Sagittarius, the big thing about this month, is we're all preparing for Mars to go retrograde on the 29th. No one likes it when Mars goes retrograde. Mars is extreme energy, physical activity and motivation. And when Mars is retrograde, it means 'lack of.' Who wants to walk around with a lack of energy, charge or motivation? Not me. Anyway, there's a higher reason to everything. Mars will be going retrograde in the sign of Pisces. Pisces is the sign that rules the mother and the home. This planetary energy will be taking place around your own mother and in your home life. The first word I receive from Spirit is 'upset.' Uranus is already moving retrograde in this area of your life, and now Mars will join. As retrograde Uranus and Mars move through your area of the home and mother, first of all, this is a time of clearing up old issues you may have with the mother, once and for all. Pluto continues to move through your Sun sign, perfecting your individuality. Right now, Pluto is also retrograde, going deep within you to find anything that may be hidden within that needs to come up, out and be faced. Retrograde Pluto will pull up old issues that connect to the mother. Face them, clear them and move on.

Spirit says that a good way of clearing issues with the mother is to clean your home. That's right! Clean your home. Retrograde Uranus and Mars moving through your home at this time says this is an awesome time to go through your home, once again, and clear out old energies. Planetary energies do not want to see us holding on to anything. So by all means, when the energy presents, move with the flow. Release the old so the new may have room to come in.

Planetary energies (the Sun, Moon, Venus, Jupiter and Mercury) are lining up heavily in the sign of Leo, placing this energy in your room of Higher Knowledge, Education and Travel. I am sure you are ready for that long-overdue trip. By all means, when the opportunity to travel presents itself, go. This will be more than just a trip. This is a learning experience. And believe me; learn as much as you can, for you will find yourself using this knowledge greatly when you return.

The Dragon's Tail continues to sweep through your room of karma, clearing the energies there. Wow! By the time Pluto finishes with Sagittarius and the Dragon's Tail is complete cleaning your room of karma, a whole new you will have emerged.

(July 2003)

CAPRICORN
DEC. 22 - JAN. 20

Capricorn, the Sun, Moon, Venus, Jupiter and Mercury are all heading towards your room of Sex, Debts and Other People's Money. An incredible opening is forming here. You are about to receive news about money that is either owed to you or money that you owe to another. This is a time of clearing your old debts and also, receiving through another. This is also a time of hearing about an inheritance or money that is destined to come to you through another.

Saturn (Lord of Karma) continues to move through the sign of Cancer, placing its energy in your room of partnership and close relationships. Saturn in Cancer is very sneaky and can be very devilish. You are about to receive a reflection of who you have been throughout the lifetime of your soul. You will find yourself, over and over again, not wanting to be a part of the relationships you are in, and some of you will leave. However, I say, hold on. Don't leave yet. You will receive a great reward from your soul, if only you face and clear this awful karma that you have created. Oh, you are probably saying, "I don't care what this says, I have never been like this..." But you know what? You have, and this is the only way you could be receiving what you are receiving this day. Quit trying to look like the victim here because you're not. What you are attracting to yourself through this other person is a direct reflection of who you once were. You may not be that person this day, however, somewhere within your souls lifetime, you have been. Now all you need to do is quit your crying and accept what has been dealt to you. Or, you could always get up and leave.

On the positive side of all this, you are being turned into a servant. In previous lifetimes of Capricorn individuals, most of you have been Kings and Queens. Most of you are coming in from lifetimes of royalty and being served by others. Well, now, this day, the shoe is on the other foot. Don't hate it. Accept it. Be the type of servant you always wanted your servants to be. Show the world how it's done. It won't be this way forever. Before you know it, you will have returned to your incredible Capricorn self, and the world will again love and accept you for the beauty you are. You have a lesson to teach to the world, and this lesson is how to be the best you can be, no matter what you are doing. Capricorns have a way of adding incredible beauty to whatever they touch. Add beauty to this situation you are in and the world will receive a great lesson.

(July 2003)

AQUARIUS
JAN. 21 - FEB. 18

Are you ready for marriage or a life-long commitment? Are you ready to become rich and famous? I tell you, with the way the planets are lining up in your room of Partnership, you are connecting with one who is incredibly talented, intelligent and good-looking. The Sun, Moon, Venus, Jupiter and Mercury will all join together in your room of Partnership this month, aligning, connecting and solidifying you with the most incredible love relationship you'll ever know.

It all began with remarkable Neptune, who has been transiting through your Sun sign for the last five years. Neptune first entered into the sign of Aquarius in late January of 1998. Ever since then, your soul has been awakening, stretching out to connect with your outer presence. Your physical shell has gone through many deaths, rebirths and changes, for it is preparing for the awakening of your soul.

Saturn is moving through the sign of Cancer in your area of health. Saturn in this area of your life will bring forth what we know as nervousness because of the changes that are occurring in your life. Try to relax and know that all is in Divine Order. At least, I hope it is for you. If your life is moving in a direction other than what is described above, know that you are out of alignment with your souls path. Perhaps you'll want to seek spiritual counseling to assist.

The Dragon's Tail continues to sweep through the sign of Scorpio in your tenth room of career / father. Many of you will go through the transformation of career and the father during this time of the Dragon's Tail sweeping through this area of your life. Many of you will go through career changes, actually doing what your soul has wanted to do for many years.

Everything in your life looks to be moving incredibly well as long you don't allow yourself to hold on to things that really need to go. Mars will be moving into retrograde position this month in your second room of material possessions, assisting you in cleaning your closets. Neptune transiting through your Sun sign is about to reveal an incredibly magnificent you. Venus, the New Moon, Jupiter and Mercury all lining up in your seventh room of partnership is creating an incredible opening for a magnificent love relationship to take place, form and solidify within your life. This is an awesome time for you.

(July 2003)

PISCES
FEB. 19 - MAR. 19

Pisces, you are the sign that represents the mother, the home and the nurturing one. Your physical body is about to go through an extreme change. The Sun, Moon, Venus, Jupiter and Mercury will all line up together in the sign of Leo, placing this energy in your room of health and the physical body. Mars will move into retrograde position in your Sun sign joining the energy of retrograde Uranus. Many of you will not be able to handle the extremities of energy here for there is a great amount of power that is preparing to be released. Mother Earth herself will also undergo extreme changes due to the abundance of activity that is about to take place. The energy of the mother is changing. You are changing. Everything as we know it to be will now change.

Many of you who have children will find this to be a very difficult and trying time, for Saturn moves through the area of the children in your life. Saturn (Lord of Karma) is moving through the sign of Cancer, placing this energy in your room of the children and family members. When your physical body goes through a lack of energy or sickness, and you find that those closest to you are not around, don't fret nor get angry. Pluto is moving through the sign of Sagittarius right now, which means "Perfect Individual." We are all going through the lessons of connecting with our perfect individuality, and this is just one of those times for you. You are being told by the powers that be to get up and stand on your own two feet and take care of yourself. We all seem to think that when we are ill, everyone has to come running to our side, especially our family members. Well, not anymore. We need to learn to run to our own side. We need to learn to take care of ourselves. We need to learn to keep the body healthy and strong so we don't get sick in the first place. Times are changing. Pluto continues to move through the sign of Sagittarius until late November 2008. Pluto is demanding that we stand strong on our own two feet and stop depending on others. What you will go through is a test of your individuality. Stand on your own two feet and care for yourself. The energy of the true mother begins to awaken.

Through this transformation the body is about to go through, an incredible amount of knowledge will be released. This knowledge is very old information that has been stored within for a very long time. This is direct information from the soul. This wealth of knowledge has to do with the healing of the land and of the physical body.

(July 2003)

ARIES
MAR. 20 - APR. 19

Aries, you are the sign that represents the child, children, child-play, fun, games, youth and creativity. The Sun, Moon, Venus, Jupiter and Mercury will all be coming into an alignment in the sign of Leo, placing this energy in your room of the children. Saturn (Lord of Karma) is presently moving through the sign of Cancer, placing its energy in your room of the Home / Mother. Uranus is presently moving retrograde in the sign of Pisces (the sign that rules the mother / home), through your area of karma. Mars will move into retrograde this month, in the sign of Pisces, also placing this energy in your area of karma. And, just what does this mean? It means that any and all of you who have things locked away inside that took place when you were a child will be activated and brought up to the surface. Your childhood is resurfacing, especially those things we wish to forget.

Are you repeating the things your mother used to say? Are you doing the things your mother used to do? Are you acting the way your mother used to act? Karma involving the mother, your childhood, your own children and your own mothering ways has come forth and is waiting for you to deal with it. Some of you will sit back and say, "Oh, not me." Well, you know what? It is you. This is the karma of the souls lifetime. Oh yeah. This is stuff your soul dished out a long time ago. Yet, you know what? Don't look at this as being bad, because it is not. We are outgrowing our old ways and habits. Even our children do not act like "children" anymore. We are rapidly advancing souls growing up (so says power of Pluto transiting through the sign of Sagittarius, perfect individual).

Your true identity will expose itself to you this month through the children. You will receive a glimpse, a vision and recognition of you through all the events that take place around you that involves the children. Where you have been, who you have been, what you have personally gone through and what you have put others through will all be exposed to you through the children. Some of you will decide to have children of your own or bring additional children into your lives. Realize that Saturn lingers nearby in the sign of Cancer, in your home. Gross events of the past will ignite within and around your home, and know, these will involve the children. Many lessons, memories and possibly fun will be brought to you through the children.

(July 2003)

TAURUS
APR. 20 - MAY 20

Taurus, you are the sign of strength, health and the builder of the land, and right now as the Dragon's Head transits through your Sun sign, the real you exposes itself in a very big way. You are not born with the power and strength you have to just sit around and twiddle your thumbs. You are born to build, to build a better body, to build a better world. And right now, the Sun, Moon, Venus, Jupiter and Mercury are all coming into an alignment in the sign of Leo, which places this energy in your room of the home, the foundation. This is a time for you to focus on the home and self. This is a time for you to pull your resources together and focus on the type of home you are to be living in at this particular time. Planetary energies say, "Build a place of knowledge." Is it a certain type of school you wish to build for the people? Is it a library? Perhaps it is some type of inspirational spiritual center to assist mankind on his journey of life. What is it you have come to build amongst this Earth? Please figure it out Taurus.

Saturn (Lord of Karma) is transiting through the sign of Cancer, placing this energy in your area of speech, communication and expression. Saturn, when placed in this area, will test what you say and how you say it to the absolute hilt. This area in which Saturn transits, is also known as the area of the talent. An idea from the past is trying to come forth and wants to be manifested through you. What is your fear Taurus? Are you afraid of the leadership responsibilities that come with this idea? Well, if so, get over it. The Dragon's Head is transiting through your Sun sign, placing this energy in your room of SELF. It's all about you finding your place within this world and doing what your soul has come here to do. Either you will do this or you won't. As the old saying goes, "Either sh--, or get off the pot."

Planetary energies are all working against you right now as far as attracting others into your life for assistance. This is because the Dragon's Head is in YOUR Sun sign. The Dragon's Head is moving through YOU, not anyone else, YOU. It's all about YOU Taurus writing out that perfect plan that YOUR soul has brought with it. And, when the time comes, energies will open up and YOU will attract the help and assistance YOU will need from others in order to manifest this plan. However, until then, this plan lays within YOU.

(July 2003)

GEMINI
MAY 21 - JUN. 20

Gemini, your work situation is about to unexpectedly change. Uranus (planet of sudden change) is moving through your area of career. Now here comes Mars (aggression). Not only has Mars crossed retrograde Uranus; Mars will go retrograde in your area of career on the 29th of this month. Saturn is moving through the sign of Cancer in your second room of money, and the Dragon's Tail is sweeping through the sign of Scorpio in your room of health and the way you work. Oh my goodness, you are about to go through an emotional down pour with what is about to take place for you in your area of career. You don't have to be so emotional about it. It's only about change. You're changing! The world is changing! Life is changing! The ways we do the things we do are changing! Get with it and change! It is only meant to make you a stronger and better person.

This change that has presented itself to you is all for the betterment of you. The Dragon's Head now moves through the sign of Taurus, placing this energy in your room of karma. The Sun, Moon, Venus, Jupiter and Mercury are all coming into an alignment in the sign of Leo, placing these energies in your room of the talent. The Dragon's Head will ignite the plan of the soul, for it is placed in the area of our life that holds the secrets of the soul. Whatever your soul has brought with it, will be expressed at this time, through the abundance of planetary energies that are lining up in your room of the talent. So you see, the only way this change that is about to take place in your area of career can catch you by surprise if you are not reading my book. I am telling you. It's no longer a surprise. Knowledge is power, you know? Knowing is 90% of our life. The other 10% is what you do with what you know.

Gemini's always want to know about personal relationships. Well, I really can't make any legitimate judgments, for you are the sign that represents partnership and close relationships. Anyway, Pluto (planet of perfection) is transiting through the sign of Sagittarius, placing its energy in your room of partnerships and close relationships. For those of you already involved in a love relationship, the partner is really about to enhance his / her individuality. For those of you who want to connect with someone, Pluto is there, and Pluto is perfection. You will either meet a perfect one or a perfect slob.

(July 2003)

Boy oh boy! You think you had it tough last year as Saturn transited above your head in the sign of Gemini, causing you to never be able to make up your mind about anything. And to think, you Cancer people surround my life. Anyway, Saturn has now moved into your first room of Self, making you check yourself a thousand times before leaving the house. Oh my God! You just can't seem to get it right, huh? Well, Saturn is doing its job. Saturn is fine-tuning you. Saturn in Cancer says "sexy," or is it slutty? Saturn in Cancer in your room of Self says, just how sexy or slutty do you need to be in order to attract the things want to attract? Some of you will go to extremes as Saturn moves through your room of the Self. Some of you will absolutely amaze yourselves with your newfound wardrobe. Saturn will take you to an extreme, one way or the other, for this is all Saturn knows.

Your outer appearance will go through a dramatic change as Saturn moves through your Sun sign. The real you will dramatically expose itself to the world. Some of you will become "sexy". Some of you will become "slutty." Just know there is a difference.

Planetary energies (the Sun, Moon, Venus, Jupiter and Mercury) are all lining up heavily in your area of money and material possessions. Now, you must know. Yes, indeed, this is a time of attracting an enormous amount of financial wealth to you; however, it all has to do with the way you dress.

The way we dress on the outside has all to do with the message we relay about the self to others. The way we dress on the outside is the expression of the soul. Now, we have already discussed Saturn moving through your area of the Self and outer appearance, bringing forth a "sexy" or "slutty" energy, right? Well, this material abundance that is destined to come your way has all to do with how you are expressing yourself on the outside. Dress like a slut, you will attract an enormous amount of money to you from someone who wants slutty service. And you know what I mean. Dress like a sexy million dollar secretary, and watch yourself attract a sexy million dollar financial opportunity. It all has to do with the way you dress, the way you express yourself on the outside. Remember, Saturn is moving through your outer appearance and will be for the next year and a half.

(July 2003)

LEO
JUL. 23 - AUG. 22

Wow! The Sun, Moon, Venus, Jupiter and Mercury will all line up in your Sun sign this month, activating and invigorating absolutely everything about you. This entire year has been about Leo's coming into their full power and this month shows it all. However, there are a few things that exist in your karmic closet that will be coming out.

Saturn (Lord of Karma) is now moving through the sign of Cancer, placing its energy in your twelfth room of karma. Saturn is activating what already exists here. Saturn in Cancer has to do with issues of sex. Let's face it. All Leos are highly motivated sexual creatures, or at least your minds are. Yes, the energy of Cancer (the sign that rules sex) lingers above your head, and not only that, Saturn is now transiting through this area of your life, triggering intense and sometimes morbid sexual thoughts.

As I look into the area of your life that rules sex, retrograde Uranus (erratic activity) and Mars (aggression) are there. Planetary energies may cause you to act out inappropriately at times, due to this incredible energy-taking place in your life. Of course there is nothing wrong with the sexual energies that exist in our life. It is when we lose control and find the self being controlled by the energy. This is when things go wrong. Just know that when the impulse hits, do something safe and legal about it.

Cancer also has to do with the energy of debt. Retrograde Uranus and Mars moving through your eighth area will also stimulate old debts. Saturn moving through the sign of Cancer in your twelfth room of karma also suggests old debt. If at all possible at this time, release yourself from material debt and karmic debt. Un-dealt with issues of the past will come around, and extremely intense at this time.

The Dragon's Tail continues to sweep through the sign of Scorpio in your area of the home. More karma being cleared. Many of you will find yourselves out of the home quite a bit, for the sweeping of the Dragon's Tail is taking place there, and the energy of the Dragon's Head is pulling you up into the outer world. Considering all of the planetary activity that is taking place in your first room of Self, and in your room of career, this is indeed a time for you to represent your Sun sign in it's absolute fullest. This is your month to shine.

(July 2003)

VIRGO
AUG. 23 - SEPT. 22

Are you ever receiving a blast from the past? The Sun, Moon, Venus, Jupiter and Mars will all align in the sign of Leo this month, placing this energy in your twelfth room of karma. Your soul holds a great deal of knowledge and information about the land. You are the sign that represents leadership to the world. What world within this world are you a leader of? Is it the world of medicine, politics, art, or religion? You are a leader, Virgo. And the reason you are such a good leader is because of the amount of knowledge your soul has gathered throughout its lifetime. You are also a traveler. You are one who will travel the land to seek out new information, because, this is what pleases your mind and soul the most. As the Sun, Moon, Venus, Jupiter and Mercury all line up in your room of karma, know that many events, circumstances, situations, issues and people will all of a sudden come around to the forefront for the issues to be rectified and cleared, once and for all.

As Saturn moves through your room of friends, you will feel as if there are many people whom you cannot trust. You may go through feelings of betrayal and loss. Saturn is the Lord of Karma, and Saturn moving through this area of your life is activating old karma amongst you and your friends. Just face it and clear it. For if you turn your back and run away from these debts you have created with other people, they will only intensify and become worse down the road. Clear them now while Saturn is on your side.

Last months messages, pertaining to relationships, were about releasing yourself from a relationship that no longer served your higher good. Uranus moved into retrograde, Mars crossed Uranus, and now later this month, Mars will go retrograde, all this activity taking place in your room of relationships. Now, just take it easy. A very dramatic and extremely intense cleansing is taking place in this area of your life. Just let it! Don't try to hang on to what no longer needs to be there. Will this person ever come back? Maybe. Only time will tell. Yet, then again, ask yourself, is that really what you want?

Allow yourself to be still and listen this month as Venus, the Sun, Moon, Jupiter and Mercury all line up in your twelfth room of karma and spirituality above your Sun. Your soul is communicating with you about what you are destined to do next. Be still and listen.

(July 2003)

LIBRA
SEP. 23 - OCT. 22

Libra, you are the sign that represents parties, social activities, friends and the gathering of many people. You are the social butterfly of the zodiac, and right now, the Sun, Moon, Venus, Jupiter and Mercury have all lined up in your eleventh room of Social and Friends, bringing to you, many people who will want you to promote something they have. Wow, you sure know how to attract a crowd.

Saturn (Lord of Karma) is moving through your room of career, in the sign of Cancer, forcing you to take a look at what you are doing in / for the world. Are you where you want to be? Are you doing what you like to do? Are you having fun with life, for this is what Libra represents to others?

The Dragon's Head is moving through your eighth room of Sex, Debts and the Partner's Resources. Are you in a place where you feel you have to financially depend on another, and is this a positive and good thing for you? Right now, as the Dragon's Tail sweeps through your area of money and finance, attracting income on your own may come as a struggle. It is definitely more in alignment for you to allow yourself to work with another, at this time. The Dragon's Tail sweeping through your area of material possessions also represents a clearing and cleansing of things you may have had around for quite some time. This is a time of allowing whom you have become to connect with another and work as a team / partnership. Yes, there will be a few challenges here and there, however, overall, you will benefit greatly from being in alignment with your soul.

Mars will go retrograde this month, in the sign of Pisces, in your room of health and the physical body. Mars and Uranus moving through this area of your life will bring about health related issues due to emotional stress. Do your best to stay strong and not allow the issues to turn into emotional issues. Much of what may be getting to you emotionally will be issues pertaining to the mother and the home. The mother's health does not look too good right now, especially if she has not taken good care of herself. Retrograde planetary energies in the sign of Pisces will weaken the energy of the mother and cause her health to rapidly deteriorate. The last thing you will want these energies to do is pull you down also. For the sake of yourself and everyone around you, be strong.

(July 2003)

SCORPIO
OCT. 23 - NOV. 21

Career is coming into an all-time high. The Sun, Moon, Venus, Jupiter and Mercury will all line up in the sign of Leo later this month, placing this intense energy in your area of career. Leo rules Higher Knowledge, Education and Travel. Many of you Scorpio individuals will find yourself traveling for work; many of you may find yourselves having to go back to school to obtain additional knowledge about what it is you're doing. Speaking of receiving additional knowledge, Saturn is right now transiting through your area of higher knowledge and travel, possibly causing you a little annoyance at times with trips you may have to take and also with knowledge you are receiving from others. Saturn is not a patient energy, especially when placed in this area of ones life. As a little precaution, do your best to stay calm when traveling, especially when driving.

The Dragon's Tail is sweeping through your identity right now, removing all that has stuck on to you that belongs to someone else. Scorpios have a way of absorbing other people's stuff, and once in a while, they need a little help shaking it off. Right now, the Dragon's Tail is major assisting you.

The Dragon's Head is moving through your room of Partnership, creating an opening for someone to enter into your life and assist you with the work you are doing, or possibly you assist another with what they are doing. Either way, a beautiful opening has been created for you and another to team up and work successfully with one another. The Dragon's Tail is sweeping through your Sun sign, one again, removing all that is not a direct reflection of you. You are becoming a whole person again. The sweeping of Dragon's Tail in your first room of Self will expose a higher, cleaner and more vibrant you by the time it completes its transit in late December 2004.

Mars moving through the sign of Pisces in your fifth room of children will join Uranus and will go retrograde at the end of the month. Mars is the planet of physical activity and aggression. Please watch the little ones around water. These planetary energies are pointing to sudden emotional disturbances pertaining to the young ones around you.

August 2003

(August 2003)

SAGITTARIUS
NOV. 22 - DEC. 21

Pluto returns direct this month, from being in retrograde position since late March. Pluto first moved into your Sun sign in mid January 1995. Pluto's job in your Sun sign is to bring forth death to the old self, so that the new self can come forth. Pluto is extreme transformation. Pluto is perfection. Your outer identity (ego) has been going through a complete overhaul ever since Pluto moved into your sign. Your soul is coming forth. Your forever-perfect soul will rise from the death of your ego. This transformation, I know, has not been an easy one. Yet, knowing that this is what your life is going through will assist you in better dealing with the things you are attracting to you.

Pluto has been working hard to shed the old. Everything you have built for yourself has now changed. Where you live, where you work, your friends and family, even the way you look and dress. Absolutely everything. As Pluto moves through your Sun sign, all that you once depended upon will go. It is time you stand on your own two feet. No more relying on mom and dad to bail you out. No more relying on your siblings or close friends to lend a helping hand. Heck, the banks may not even want to loan money to you. Pluto in Sagittarius says independence, stand on your own two feet and figure it out, once and for all, for yourself.

Planetary energies suggest that an incredible job opportunity, advancement or promotion will be taking place for you within this month. However, Mercury will go retrograde, delaying the decision. If this is something you really want, and it will be, you will have to put forth your absolute best in order to get it. Pluto returns direct the day after Mercury goes retrograde, blessing you with the power you will need in order to put forth your best. Your hair, your clothes, your nails, your shoes, your jewelry, your accessories, your makeup. Absolutely everything that has to do with the outer appearance must radiate the soul. Remember, as Pluto moves through your Sun sign, your old ways are dying and the soul is coming forth. The soul is totally perfect, so therefore, the outer must find a way to present the soul. This is the only way you will attract this grand opportunity to you. This grand opportunity that has to do with finding your place within this world, is indeed something the soul has attracted to it. Now, the mind must figure out a way to align with soul and make this opportunity yours.

(August 2003)

CAPRICORN
DEC. 22 - JAN. 20

This person you have pulled into your life continues to be a challenge, yet this is karma you are dealing with. Saturn, Lord of Karma, continues to transit through your opposing room of the partner (those closest to you), making it very challenging, and sometimes difficult, to deal with the situations of others. The energy of Saturn says, reflection. What you are pulling to you through others is a direct of reflection of whom you have been. Many of you will deny it, however, fact is fact.

This is a very good time of year for Capricorns to do a little traveling, and possibly getting away from those challenges with other people. But, guess what? Wherever you go, there will be "other people," and guess what else? You may just have to talk to them. Oh boy, what a chore. Can you imagine? (Smile)

Mercury will go retrograde this month, in your area of travel, possibly causing a delay or two with travel plans. Don't worry, it is meant to happen this way.

Virgo is the sign that rules your area of Higher Knowledge, Education and Travel. Capricorn people do well in jobs that have to do with the entertainment, teaching and assisting of many people (such as travel guide / flight attendant, Hotel Management, Night Club owner / operator, interior designers, clothes designer, makeup artist). These are just a few that come to mind. Anyway, my point in acknowledging this information to you is because of the planetary alignment that is about to take place in this area of your life. Something new will open up, and it will have something to do with the above-described jobs. However, Mercury is there also, and will be going retrograde (reverse) this month, causing whatever is destined to take place, to be held up for a while. The reason is because some of you will need to decide whether or not you want this change.

Pluto, planet of transformation and perfection, will also be going direct this month, in the sign of Sagittarius, in your twelfth room of karma. You are about to receive a glimpse of your higher self, what he / she looks like, and what he / she is doing. Pluto in Sagittarius says "Perfect Individual," at least; this is what we will be as soon as Pluto completes its transit in Sagittarius.

(August 2003)

AQUARIUS
JAN. 21 - FEB. 18

Planetary energies are lining up in your area of Sex, Debts and the Partners' Resources suggesting that someone, could be a close friend or intimate partner, will present you with an incredible job / work opportunity. This opportunity is one that is destined to approach you at this particular time in your life. Since the Tail of the Dragon is sweeping through your area of career at this time, it looks as is this opportunity is something you will be able to do from the comfort of your own home. Some of you who are married or in a committed relationship will receive this offer through your partner. For those of you who are not in a committed relationship, this offer will come in through a friend or associate. However, something is destined to come in at this time, that is, if you are walking in alignment with the will of your soul, your Divine energy source.

Mercury will go retrograde this month in the sign of Virgo, placing this energy in your area of Sex and Debts, in other words, the room of other's people 'stuff.' Mercury going retrograde in this area will present a temporary change in plans. First of all, do you owe money to anyone? If so, this Mercury retrograde will place a delay on repayment of the debt. Don't sweat it. If at this time, you just don't have what you promised to have, bring forth the power of the voice and communicate the truth to the one you owe. They will understand. Another situation you may attract to you through this Mercury retrograde is, someone may present to you a plan, suggestion or idea, and then walk away because they're not sure about one thing or another. Just hang in there. All will work out as it is intended to go.

Some of you may be feeling a little anxious / desperate for money to come in. Uranus and Mars are both moving retrograde (reverse) in your area of material possessions and finance, actually pulling money and material items away from you. First of all, it's time to get rid of stuff. Aquarians have a way of collecting stuff from other people, and not knowing when to get rid of it. Well, now is a very good time to eliminate this stuff. Retrograde Uranus and Mars are not easy energies to deal with. Together, they mark a time of intense elimination. Right now, while they are moving in retrograde position, their energies are actually relaxed, giving you a chance to clean out your closets all on your own before the planets return direct and do it for you.

(August 2003)

PISCES
FEB. 19 - MAR. 19

Your life is headed towards a serious commitment between yourself and another. Jupiter, planet of abundance, moves into the sign of Virgo this month, your opposing sign, placing its energy in your room of partnership and close relationships. Not only that, Venus, planet of love, beauty and attraction, will also be entering into this area of your life. Yet, you know who else is there, Mercury, planet of communication. Mercury will be moving into retrograde this month, causing the partner to possibly consider proposing to you, however, maybe pulling back, making sure this is what he /she really wants. Now, just relax. This person just wants to make sure this is the right thing to do.

Some of you will attract a beautiful job proposition to you. Yet, then again, Mercury will be moving retrograde this month, and the other person may just sit back for a while and think on it, making sure you're the right person for the job.

So, let's say this is something you really want. Now, just what will you need to do to make sure you get it? Right now, Pluto is moving through your area of career (your place / standing in the world) in the sign of Sagittarius. Pluto in Sagittarius says "Perfect Individual." You will need to come into a complete alignment with Pluto in Sagittarius (which is perfection) in order to attract this opportunity to you. Just how "bad" do you want this? Just how far will you go to make sure this opportunity is yours? Pluto will take you from one extreme to the next. Choose carefully the direction you desire to precede, for this choice will be with you for the rest of your life.

Many of you Pisces individuals will decide to have children at this time in your life, yet, guess what? Please go with the flow of what you are really feeling. Saturn is moving through your area of children until July of 2005. Giving birth at this time is not advisable for Saturn will bring forth the most intense souls there are to deal with. And don't be one of those stupid Pisces people walking around saying "Well, if it's God's intention for me to have a child at this time, then so be it." Because you know what? You are God, and you are the one in charge of your own life, destiny and fate. So don't go blaming some entity you have never seen on the decisions you make. If you get pregnant at this time, it is by the choice of YOU.

(August 2003)

ARIES
MAR. 20 - APR. 19

Have you thought about doing work in / with the health care industry? Planetary energies will be lining up in the sign of Virgo in your room of health, suggesting that for some of you, work in the health care industry will become available. However, Mercury, planet of communication, also transiting through this area, will be going retrograde at the end of the month, wavering your decision a bit. This is just not the time for you to decide one way or the other. Use this time during Mercury retrograde to weigh the pros and cons of the situation. And by the time Mercury returns direct, the decision should be clearer.

For you others, these planetary energies will have to do with other types of work you are doing. These energies are actually enhancing your workload quite a bit, and the physical body. Jupiter, planet of abundance, is moving through your area of the physical body, so if you're not looking to put on a few extra pounds, you might want to take it easy at the dinner table. Anyway, your health actually looks pretty good, even for those of you who have had health difficulties in the past.

From October 2001 through April 2003, the Dragon's Head moved through your room of speech, communication, expression and the talent. During this time, a suggestion, plan, idea was brought to you through one who exudes a strong individual stance within this world, in other words a very unique person. Did you listen? Did you pay attention to what this person suggested you do? Are you doing it? Well if so, the Dragon's Head has now moved into your area of money and material gain, representing that if you followed the advice that was given to you, you will now be in a position of receiving greatly from the Universe for doing exactly what your soul is destined to be doing. You no longer should be going through your fight with life. Love, which is the soul in action, should have materialized right before your face. The many things you have wanted to do, the many places you have wanted to visit, the many items you have wanted to purchase are all available to you, now, just for allowing your soul to live. You see, it "pays" to listen.

(August 2003)

TAURUS
APR. 20 - MAY 20

This month brings about a particular debt your soul owes to a particular female child. This child may not be a child at all, yet this will be one who is quite younger than you.

Spirit shows me that many of you Taurus individuals are working on a specific career plan / goal for yourself, and for more reasons than one, this particular plan just doesn't seem to manifest. Well, right now, the Dragon's Tail is sweeping through the sign of Scorpio, in your area of partnership and close relationships. Scorpio is the sign of karma, and for many of you, the Dragon's Tail is bringing forth old karmic debts your soul owes to another. For many of you this debt will be to an old lover; to others, your child or someone else's child. Yet, for all of you, this person is female. Pluto will return direct this month in your area of Debts, in the sign of Sagittarius. Again Taurus, there is a particular debt your soul is readying to pay to particular female person, one younger than yourself. Your soul promised to assist this person in finding her individuality within this world. Now, is the time to do so. Spirit says that you will recognize who this person is.

You have been so focused on yourself lately, and on the things YOU want to do. Well, guess what? Your higher self says it is all about you, yet, in a different way. It is all about you assisting another in reaching "her" higher place within this world. This is just something your soul promised to do, and now the time is here for you to do this.

Saturn, Lord of Karma, is presently moving through the sign of Cancer, placing its energy in your room of speech, communication, expression and the talent. Again, spirit shows us that there is a karmic debt your soul needs to express at this time. Saturn can get anxious at times and will present something to be more than it really is, or will rush through it just to have it "done." Whatever you are working on, please take your time and fine-tune it every step of the way. Remember, you are dealing with Saturn, Lord of Karma, and if you half-do your job, it will come back around to haunt you, intensely. Yet, you know what? I trust that you will use the energy of Saturn transiting through your room of speech, communication, expression and the talent to carry out this plan in its absolute highest. I just know you will.

(August 2003)

GEMINI
MAY 21 - JUN. 20

Planetary energies are focusing on the home / mother in your life.

First of all, there is a new place of residence or an enhancement within the home you are presently in. Jupiter moves into the sign of Virgo this month, placing this energy into your home / living space. Jupiter brings forth great enhancements. Not only is Jupiter there, Venus, planet of love, beauty and attraction is there also. This is an absolutely incredible time for Gemini's right now; for it looks as if you are finally moving into the home you have often dreamed of. You see? Dreams do come true. Do not allow your mind to worry if the plans pertaining to this new home do not go according to schedule, for Mercury, moving through this area also, will go retrograde this month, allowing you time to fine-tune the details. Do not panic. Everything is going according to plan, just not your plan. Mercury returns direct September 20th, showing you that all is fine and in accordance.

Pluto returns direct this month in the sign of Sagittarius, in your room of Partnership and Close Relationships. The partner is finally getting himself / herself together. Pluto in Sagittarius says, "Perfect Individual." During the last few years, the partner has gone through a complete transformation of the self. Now, planetary energies show that the partner has become a very strong individual, and is ready to bestow his / her blessings upon you. Open your hands.

Saturn continues it's transit through your room of money and material possessions, representing that this is a time where you might want more than you can afford. Remember that new home that spirit spoke about earlier? Well, you'll want to do a lot more shopping than you might be able to afford. Beeeeeeeeee careful with this energy, for sometimes Saturn will want something sooooooooo badly, he may just go out and "take" it, feeling as if what he's taking is rightfully his. Don't let this negativity of Saturn get to you. Stay in the highest. When the timing is right, you will have whatever it is you are desperately wanting now. Remember, Saturn is Lord of Karma, and considering the way the energies are right now, if you steal, you'll get caught right away. Some of you will go overboard at this time, spending all the cash that is available to you and charging your credit cards to the max. There is always a light to every situation. I suppose the light in this situation is you're making creditors rich.

(August 2003)

CANCER
JUN. 21 - JUL. 22

Jupiter (planet of wealth, abundance and expansion) will be moving into the sign of Virgo (career and your standing in the world) later this month, activating your talent and gift to the world. Congratulations Cancer!!! You are finally receiving an acknowledgement of who you are and why you are here.

Right now, the Dragon's Tail is sweeping through the sign of Scorpio, which represents karma. The Tail is sweeping through your room of children. Spirit says that many of you, at this time, will go through a remembering of what you said you wanted to be and do when you were a child. Childhood memories are being released through the sweeping of the Dragon's Tail. You are finally connecting with what you are here to do in this world. I am very happy for you.

Saturn is moving through your Sun sign, activating your charm and sexual power. Yet, it's not a physical sexual power, it a spiritual sexual power. This is an orgasmic energy that is coming from a level much, much higher than the physical. You are connecting with your power. Your outer personality has come into a higher alignment with Saturn, and now you will attract incredible opportunities to you. Not only do you have the power of Saturn on your side, you also have Pluto in Sagittarius, (which means "Perfect Individual") moving through your room of health and the physical body. Pluto will return direct this month, enhancing, even more, your physical body and outer characteristics.

Planetary energies (the upcoming New Moon, Venus, Jupiter and Mercury) are all lining up in your area of the talent. An incredible talent is about to expose itself this month; something you will want to do as your career. However, Mercury will move into retrograde position on the 28th causing much doubt to come forth. This is retrograde Mercury's job. "Let me think about", says Mercury retrograde, and this is exactly what you are to be doing at this time. Fine-tuning your presentation so that when Mercury returns direct on the 20th of September, you will be totally ready to present your thing. Practice makes perfect. Use this time of Mercury going retrograde to practice and perfect whatever it is you are working on. You will do very well.

(August 2003)

LEO
JUL. 23 - AUG. 22

It's all about work, career and money. As Jupiter moved through your Sun sign, you were presented an opportunity to bring forth your best. Jupiter is the planet of abundance, expansion, wealth and growth. This month you will receive a reflection of whom you have become through the wealth that is destined to come your way.

Jupiter will move into the sign of Virgo later this month, placing its energy in your room of material possessions. Yes, that's correct. Jupiter is about to enter into your area of personal property, finances, money and material gain. What you receive will be a reflection of who you are. A man's character is measured by his wealth. This is one of the oldest sayings ever, yet, will remain true throughout this lifetime. Planetary energies are lining up heavily in your room of money and personal property, all symbolic of which you have become. The Dragon's Head continues to move through the sign of Taurus, in your room of career, letting us know that this is a time where a dream becomes a reality.

This plan you have been working with or doing is a plan of the soul. The Dragon's Tail sweeping through the sign of Scorpio (karma), in your area of the home lets us know that the home of the past (your childhood) held the memory of your identity. Many will tell us to go back to our childhood and remember what it was we said we would do when grew up. Well, for you Leo, this stands very true. Many of you are finding yourself doing what you once pretended to do when you were a child. Many of you are finding an incredible success with what you are doing. Many of you will not let this incredible energy end here, for you will allow yourself to continue to perfect the self and become better and better each day.

Pluto returns direct this month in your area of the children, activating your individuality through the young ones around you. A strong message for many of you Leo people who might be having a hard time figuring out who you are, see yourself through the children, for it will be through those younger than yourself where you will see a reflection of your perfect individuality.

(August 2003)

VIRGO
AUG. 23 - SEPT. 22

Jupiter has been moving through the sign of Leo, in your room of karma, activating your souls higher knowledge. Jupiter has also brought forth events, situations and people from your past. Your life is destined for you and another to walk, work, live and love side by side. This is your place within the world, like the President of the United States, he and his partner, whether this is the Vice President or his wife, to walk side by side. You, Virgo, are the president of your world. What is it you are in charge of? Come into your power Virgo, and be the leader you are destined to be.

Later this month, Jupiter will move into your Sun sign, expanding your power and energies in the world. Spirit says that first the work will be done on the Self. There is quite a bit of cleansing you will need to go through, considering last month, many of you went through relationship transformations, and now this month, you will need to cleanse yourself of those energies. Getting rid of the past, freeing yourself from the binds that have kept you from being you. Many of you Virgo individuals are coming out of karmic relationships where you were the parent. This was your karma. I hope you did the best you could do with that situation so that the past does not have to come back around.

You will find yourself going through moments of loneliness and sadness, for Mercury will go retrograde later this month in your Sun sign. Just do the best you can do with the energies that present them to you. Right now, it is all about you cleansing yourself of the energies of the past, for a new you are preparing to come forth as Jupiter steps into your Sun sign and does its thing.

Pluto will go direct in the area of your home on the 29th. Pluto is moving through the sign of Sagittarius, which represents "Perfect Individual." This is a time for you to recognize and become one with your perfect individuality. You may find yourself alone and feeling rather lonely, yet this is the way it is meant to be. Your soul needs to cleanse itself of the events it has recently gone through. You have just gone through an incredible karmic experience, one that may take several months to clear. Yet, for some of you, even longer. Yet, it won't be this way forever. What you need to clear will one day, eventually, be cleared.

(August 2003)

LIBRA
SEP. 23 - OCT. 22

Jupiter, the New Moon and Venus are all headed towards your room of karma, as Mercury, planet of communication, prepares to go retrograde there. Saturn, Lord of Karma, is currently transiting through the sign of Cancer, in your room of career. The Dragon's Tail is currently sweeping through the sign of Scorpio (karma) in your room of money and material possessions. A way in which your soul used to work and make its money is about to come up and out to the surface. This may be something you were involved in within this lifetime, or a lifetime ago.

Planetary energies are lining up and moving towards your room of karma in the sign of Virgo. Virgo rules career, letting us know that a job situation of the past is coming back around. When we look into your area of career, we have the planet Saturn (lord of karma) moving through the sign of Cancer (sex). Yes, this job situation of the past exudes a strong sexual energy. When we look into your area of Sex, there exists the Dragon's Head in the sign of Taurus, as the Tail sweeps through the sign of Scorpio (karma) in its opposite room of money and material receiving. Here is nothing to be ashamed of nor frightened of, or other. This is just something that is. Many Libra people have been "pimps and hookers" in their previous lifetime. As the Dragon's Tail sweeps through the sign of Scorpio, many secrets of the past will come up and out. There will be no more secrets when the tail gets through with the sign of Scorpio (late December 2004).

Libra is a very social sign. It is the sign that represents the gathering of many people. And when many people begin to gather, sexual energy and attraction sometimes takes place.

You will face, this month, through yourself and through others around you, a deep reflection of your past, whether this is the past of this lifetime, or a past lifetime. Sexual energy is radiating all around you, everywhere you go and through many you meet. It is the energy of Saturn in Cancer. Do your best to maintain perspective and don't allow your mind to get lost in the moment of the energy, for the energy will become very intense. Stay in control.

(August 2003)

SCORPIO
OCT. 23 - NOV. 21

Planetary energies are lining up in the sign of Virgo (career), placing this energy in your room of Friends and Social activities. Many, many people will soon gather around you, especially women. It is information they will seek from you. Do you have it to give?

Leo is the sign that represents higher knowledge and education. Leo is the energy that rules your area of career, your place in this world. Scorpio is the sign of karma, old soul, and one from the past, one whose soul has been around for a very long time. Within the being of the Scorpio exists a wealth of ancient knowledge and information. These many women who are about to find their way to you are in need of this information, for they wish to know what is going on with them, and you have the answer. You know why you'll have the answer? Because your soul has already experienced everything these people are now going through. You, Scorpio, are receiving a reflection of you through these many women.

Saturn is presently moving through your area of information, in the sign of Cancer. Cancer rules the energy of giving; learning to give appropriately without taking away the power of another. Here we have Saturn (lord of karma) in Cancer in your room of Higher Knowledge, representing that your life is destined to sharing higher knowledge and information to the people of this world. Your job as a Scorpio is to feed knowledge to the people. Yet, Mercury will go retrograde this month, in the sign of Virgo, in your room of other people. Know that it is okay if you just don't have it to give at this moment. Move with the flow of the planetary energies. Mercury will return direct September 20.

Pluto returns direct on the 29th of this month. Right now, Pluto is moving through the sign of Sagittarius, in your room of money and material possessions. The Universe wishes to bless you with the finest treasures of the land. However, since Pluto is transiting through the sign of Sagittarius, you will need to perfect your individuality in the absolute highest (for this is what Pluto in Sagittarius means), in order to attract the highest. Pluto transiting through the room of money and material possessions brings forth the finest treasures of the land. However, in order for one to attract the finest treasures of the land, one must become a fine treasure of the land.

September 2003

(September 2003)

SAGITTARIUS
NOV. 22 - DEC. 21

This is a very positive month for you, Sag. The New Moon will take place in your room of friends and social, making this a time of connecting with those whom you may not have seen in a while, and connecting with new people. Pluto has gone direct, your energy is stronger and you seem to be feeling really good about yourself.

Mercury (planet of communication) will return direct on the 20th in the sign of Virgo, in your room of career. Things are really beginning to look up for you. Jupiter (planet of abundance) is also moving through your area of career, enhancing whatever you are doing, possibly, bringing forth something totally new for you to do. I remember last month, it looked as if a job opportunity had approached you, yet the decision was delayed. Well, this month, it looks as if you got that new job / promotion, and it also looks as if you are enjoying the many new people who are coming into your life. I tell you; Pluto can really wreak havoc in one's life, especially if one is not aware of what's going on.

Mars returns direct on the 27th in the sign of Pisces, placing its energy in your room of Home / Mother. Some of us went through excruciating emotional drama pertaining to the home and mother, several months ago, when Uranus and Mars went into retrograde mode. Uranus continues to move in retrograde direction, yet its energy has now moved back into the sign of Aquarius, placing its energy in your room of speech, communication and expression. Is there something you may have forgotten to say? For those of you who may be going through emotional drama with the mother, use this time to say the things that really need to be said, because for many of us, the mother won't be around for much longer.

Saturn continues to move through the sign of Cancer in your room of Debts. Planetary energies are asking those of you who have outstanding debts to please recognize them and pay them, so that this energy can be released from you. Pluto moving through your Sun sign at this time wants to move about freely and happily without all those karmic restrictions. Connect with your true individuality and face your karmic debts. Really, you'll feel so much better when you do.

(September 2003)

CAPRICORN
DEC. 22 - JAN. 20

A new job situation looks to have presented itself to you last month. This month looks like the position has been accepted, however, the type of money you are promised to receive will be received later. Something looks more like commission. The more people you connect with and the more sales you make, the more money you will make. Speaking a little more on money, investment opportunities look to be held up, however, just wait. They will begin to pay off very soon.

Mars returns direct on the 27th of this month, in the sign of Pisces, in your room of Communication. Is there something you need to say? Well, if so, you will have Mars on your side to say whatever needs to be said. Just remember, things do have a way of coming back around. Make sure that what you do say to another is said in its highest.

Other people may continue to be a challenge for you with the Dragon's Tail sweeping through your room of other people and Saturn transiting through your room of partnership. Any way you look at it right now, there are intense differences with other people. Well, this has to do with your prejudice. That's right. Many Capricorn people can be very prejudice against difference. It's just who you are. And you know what else? Right now, everything you are attracting to you through others is something you have judged incorrectly at one time and another. I know, right now, many of you are probably sitting and reading this and saying, "I'm not prejudice. I love black people." You see how limited your mind vocabulary can be. Look up the word prejudice and open your mind. Everything you don't like will all of a sudden be brought before you just so you can find the "like" in it.

Planetary energies are making it very possible for you to get away for a while, or maybe permanently. Jupiter and Mercury are both moving through your room of Higher Knowledge and Travel, creating an opening for you to get away. Some of this getting way will have to do with career, for these energies are taking place in the sign of Virgo, which rules the energy of career. Well, whatever these travel opportunities bring for you Capricorn, enjoy them.

Mars will return direct this month in your area of communication. Watch what you say. Mars is incredible power, and through Mars' energy, you will express yourself directly. Just take your time.

(September 2003)

AQUARIUS
JAN. 21 - FEB. 18

Looks like several of you are going on your honeymoon. Planetary activity suggests lots of sex and lots of travel. Jupiter (planet of abundance) is now transiting through your eighth room of Sex, enhancing the intimacy between you and another; at least I hope it's with another. You never know. One thing I do know is Jupiter moved through your area of partnership from August of 2002 through August of 2003, creating a huge opening for someone to come into your life and connect with you on a life long basis. Now, whether or not you let someone in is totally up to you. Another thing I know is Jupiter has now moved into your eighth room of sex, activating those hormones. If you decided to not allow anyone to come into your life while Jupiter transited your room of partnership, you're really missing out.

Mars will return direct on the 27th of this month, placing its energy in your room of money and material gain. Open up your hands, it's time for you to receive. Not only that, it looks like mom's cleaning out the closets and wants to give a lot of her stuff to you. This is also very symbolic, you know? Well, if that's what you want...

Looking into the area of career, the Dragon's Tail continues to sweep there, in the sign of Scorpio, clearing out the old, so that what the soul is destined to do can come forth and be done. The message I receive for you is something you have wanted to do for a very long time is finally being made possible for you to do. And considering that the Dragon's Head is moving through the sign of Taurus in your area of the home, it looks as if this long time dream will be manifested.

I am very pleased with you Aquarius, for I know many of you went through crap in the last few years, trying desperately to figure out your place within this world. Finally, planetary energies are making it very possible for you to do what you soul is destined to be doing.

A little extra cash comes in this month, however just wait. Uranus returns direct in November, and will move back into the sign of Pisces in late December, placing its energy in your room of money and material receiving. Depending upon how well you do with Uranus' final cleansing of the self, has all to do with 'how much' more you will receive. Just put forth your best, do your best, be you best, and you will attract the best. Get ready to step forth into a new world.

(September 2003)

PISCES
FEB. 19 - MAR. 19

And just what is this I see? A proposal? You bet it is. At least it is for some of you. Planetary energies are suggesting the connecting, aligning and solidifying of a relationship. Jupiter has moved into your room of Partnership, creating a huge opening for many of you to attract an incredible love relationship into your life. The New Moon and Venus will take place in your room of Sex, Debts and Partner's Resources, indicating a beautiful gift of love is coming your way, through one you are very close to, and considering that these planetary energies are lining up in the sign of Libra, you can expect to receive MANY gifts from the one who loves you. All in all, planetary energies are showing us that an incredible love relationship is taking place for Pisces people, and I feel each one of you deserve it. Many of you will pull this expression of love to you through your children.

Saturn is moving through your area of the children / family members. Let's hope you're not pregnant at this time. This is the last thing you will want to do with Saturn moving through this area of your life. Believe me, you will give birth to karma himself. Everything you've ever said or did that has not been in the highest will be reflected a thousand times over through this child you bring in through Saturn. (Some of you are already going through this with the children / you already have.) However, just wait if you can. Saturn will move out of this area in your life in July of 2005. For those of you who are already dealing with rebelliousness through your children, it's karma.

Pisces is the sign that represents the mother, and right now, our world is going through extreme anguish with our children. Many of them are acting out and rebelling against the ways of the mother, and many parents will not be able to handle these extreme messages and lessons and will lose control. Hang in there. These young ones are actually trying to give us a message about the way we parent. Our children of this day no longer want to be treated like children. These souls are letting us know that they have been around before, and no one owns them. Let's hope we as a parenting world will learn this lesson we are being taught through our children and will allow ourselves to be the more evolved parent. Actually, we have no choice. We will evolve into a higher state of parenting. You can either jump on the boat, or stay behind. As always, the choice to live is always our own.

(September 2003)

ARIES
MAR. 20 - APR. 19

A time comes around where you fall in love, meet someone new, or perhaps, learn a little bit more on how to appreciate the one you are with. The New Moon and Venus are headed towards your room of partnership and close relationships, stimulating what's already there, or perhaps creating an opening for a new love relationship to come in.

Aries, you are the sign that represents the children of our world, and as we look this day at those we call our children, we see that they're not so "young" at all. Truly, within the bodies of these children, are older, divine, wise and intelligent beings. These children have rebelled against their parents, letting us know that they will not stand to be treated the way our parents treated us. Saturn now moves through the sign of Cancer, placing this energy in your room of the Home and Mother. Saturn (Lord of Karma) is bringing back to you, old, un-dealt with issues of the mother, or perhaps, your own mothering issues. Mars, right now, moves through the sign of Pisces (the mother), in your room of karma (your spiritual closet), once again, bringing back past issues related to the mother. This is a time for you to come face to face with your old, undealt with issues pertaining to the mother. This is also a message for the children and the child within. Mars and Saturn are both presenting to us a time where the child will face its fears of the mother, and once and for all, clear them. Venus moves into your room of close relationships, this is an optimum time to cleanse with love.

The Dragon's Tail continues to sweep through your room of debts, in the sign of Scorpio (karma), assisting you in clearing old debts and karma you may have with others. The Dragon's Head slowly moves through your room of receiving right now, in the sign of Taurus, bringing forth reward to you for clearing your debts. You see how the system works? Pay your debts. Do what is necessary and appropriate of you to do and don't worry about what you're going to get back What you put out to another, will multiply and return back to you.

Jupiter now moves through your room of health and the physical body, in the sign of Virgo (career), attracting to you a ton of work and things to do. The last couple of years were a time of preparation and perfection of your trade. This is a time where you will attract much business to you, that is, if your trade is in the highest order.

(September 2003)

TAURUS
APR. 20 - MAY 20

Taurus, this month is all about your health, physical body and the way you work. Many of you may decide to do a few extra things to keep your physical body in tiptop shape and working order. Planetary influences suggest a bit of physical motivation and exercise. Perhaps there will be a desire to eat better and get more rest and fresh air. Whatever it is you decide to do pertaining to the health of your physical body looks like you will be doing this with another.

Mars returns direct this month in your area of friends and social, bringing forth a friendly young male, one who is rather nurturing and likes to cook. This young males energy also looks to be the one whom you'll be getting some additional exercise with.

According to the messages of the planets, social activities have been a little drawn lately. Not a lot going on for you in the outside world. That's because your inside world (home, mother, family members and relatives) has been pulling most of your energy, attention and focus. There has been quite a bit of planetary activity taking place there. Right now, Jupiter, planet of abundance, continues its transit through your room of siblings and family members, continuing to bring forth quite a bit of work there with the children and members of your family. Most of what needs to take place here is communication. Looks like everyone needs to talk or at least be talked to.

Right now, in your area of communication, Saturn (Lord of Karma) transits there. Are there any old promises you may have made a long time ago? Well, if so, this is the time of old promises coming back around, and many having to do with your family members. Saturn will also test you with the words you use this day. Think carefully before speaking, for whatever you say can and will be held against you in someone else's mind. Be careful of what you say to another.

Taurus people are continuing to go through a time of karmic repayment. Whatever you have done to another will indeed come back around at this time. The Dragon's Tail is sweeping through the sign of Scorpio right now, sweeping through the past and karma of us all. For you, this energy is sweeping through your room of partnerships and close relationships, bringing back the past. Whatever it is you need to clear in this area, clear it. You'll feel so much better when you do.

(September 2003)

GEMINI
MAY 21 - JUN. 20

Planetary energies are pulling you into the home. As the Dragon's Tail sweeps through your room of health, in the sign of Scorpio, old health related issues would resurface. Old un-dealt with issues will come up at this time, through the physical body, especially health issues that never really totally went away. This could be why planetary energies are pulling you into the home. Perhaps this is a time of rest, healing and prayer. The Dragon's Head is moving through your room of karma and spirituality, pulling much of your energies into that space, letting you know that this is a time of prayer, mediation and connecting with your God source and spirituality. As the Dragon's Head moves through your room of karma and spirituality, your higher self is asking to connect with you. Your soul is attempting to connect with your mind, and sometimes, when the soul wants to connect with the mind, it will shut down or slow down the physical body just so you'll listen. This is a time of receiving many messages from the heavens, from your higher self, about you and your path. Who are you and what are you here to do? This is what your soul is attempting to relay to you. If you feel your body feeling sick or lack of energy, stop for moment, rest and listen to the voice of God. This is a time where your higher self is reaching out to connect with you.

Mars returns direct this month in the sign of Pisces, placing this energy in your room of career. Many of you are about to switch roles. Last year you may have found yourself working for a huge company, when this year you'll find yourself working for you. Many of you supported the partner, when now the partner will support you. Whatever your case may be, you are about to find yourself doing the exact opposite of what you have been doing. It time for a switch. Many of you, in the last couple of years, found yourselves taking care of the partner and being the strong one in the relationship, for the Dragon's Tail was sweeping through your room of partnership, sweeping through the identity, the money and everything else of the partner. Many of your partners became ill, were possibly out of work, or working a job that wasn't to their fullest potential. Well, the Dragon's Tail has moved on, and now the partner "should" be more into his / her fuller power. You know the old saying, "what goes around, comes around?" Well, let's hope you did your best when it came to your personal relationship. For truly, what took place last year is about to switch. What goes around comes around.

(September 2003)

CANCER
JUN. 21 - JUL. 22

Planetary energies are lining up around your home, mother and family members. You will either be moving into a new home this month, redecorating the one you already have, visiting your mother and family members or having a huge party. As the Sun prepares to move into the sign of Libra, a time of socializing and fun prevails. There is definitely something on your agenda to be celebrated.

Mars returns direct this month, assisting you in making plans for travel. Again, this energy is taking place in the sign of Pisces, suggesting that this trip has to do with visiting the mother, the home or family members who live in a different town or state. Whatever it is you have been working on really looks to be taking off in a very positive way. I feel you are finally coming into your own.

Many of you went through a time of disconnecting from the home and mother, whether this was your mother, grandmother, your own mothering ways and habits, etc. A time of releasing yourself from the energies of the mother and home were upon you last year and earlier this year. It was a time for you to step out and allow yourself to find yourself. Most of you did an exceptionally wonderful job of releasing. However, many of you are not so sure. I can see you are still questioning whether or not you made the right choice.

Saturn has been moving though your Sun sign since June of this year, and will be with you until July 2005. Saturn is strengthening your identity. Saturn is assisting you in finding your true self, discovering your true path. For so long, you have been walking around taking care of everyone else, feeling like the parent to all. Well, now that Saturn has moved into your Sun sign, you are now questioning your place. This sense of freedom has suddenly come upon you and you want to go and be free without feeling responsible for someone else. Yet know, it is good to question. It is good to have doubt. It is good to go back and forth; for this is the only way you'll ever get it right. Sometimes, we do need to detach and step outside of a situation, for this is the only way we can see how best handle it. Saturn will bring forth feelings of doubt, guilt and question. It's all right if Saturn's energy gets you down; just don't let it keep you down. By the time Saturn is through with your Sun sign, you will have found perfection with you.

(September 2003)

LEO
JUL. 23 - AUG. 22

Your mind and body are bursting with new plans and ideas all over the place. There is a lot you want to do, and believe me; looks like you're going to do it all. Mars returns direct this month on the 27th, in the sign of Pisces, in your room of Sex, Debts and Other People's Money. Looks like someone is about to connect with you about a plan or idea you may have. Your mind is bursting with ideas all over the place, and it looks as if you have shared much of what you want to do with someone else, one who actually likes your idea and wants to monetarily support it. Wow! Are you blessed! I feel that this person coming into your life, connecting with you on a plan you have, is someone who will remind you of your mother.

Leo people are going through karmic clearance pertaining to the mother, the home you grew up in and your own mothering abilities. The Dragon's Tail is sweeping through the sign of Scorpio (karma), in your room of home and the mother. Old karmic issues and remembrances of the mother and the homes you grew up in are coming up and out through the energy of the Dragon's Tail. There's a part of you that feels as if your mom did not give to you the way you thought she should. These old memories and feelings will resurface for the sake of being dealt with and cleared. Take a look at who you are this day. Do you like what you see? If not, change it into something you do like. Your mother (grandmother, father, aunt, uncle, etc., whoever was the nurturing one in your life) did what she knew to do at that particular time. Everything you attracted to yourself was all for the betterment of the self. The more you learn to love and appreciate the one who presented a mothering ness in your life, the happier of a person you become. With Saturn lingering over your head right now, messing with your thoughts, I am sure some of the thoughts and memories you are having are not all pleasant. Take a deep breath, release and let go. Okay, so it's not that easy. Yet, then again, it is. Face whatever fears may be haunting you. Scream their name out loud. Let this energy know you are not afraid of facing it.

A lot of who you are now, a lot of whom you have been in lifetimes before, a lot of who you are destined to be will be seen through your family members or those younger than yourself. Don't be afraid to allow yourself to see the beauty in others. For what you do see in another is really a reflection of you.

(September 2003)

VIRGO
AUG. 23 - SEPT. 22

Virgo, I am really happy to see such beautiful things beginning to blossom for you. Your Sun sign has gone through quite a transformation, and it is good to see you still standing. Much of what you went through was your own karma, and once in a while, the Universe has a way of bringing the past back around, for us to face and clear. Do you think we'll ever get it right?

Jupiter (planet of abundance, expansion and financial wealth and growth) is transiting through your Sun sign until September of 2004, expanding your identity. You are coming into a time of strong individuality. Jupiter will take you through few ups and downs, only so a stronger you can come forth. Like the old saying goes, "What doesn't kill you only makes you stronger." Yep, this phrase is a perfect description of Jupiter moving through your Sun sign.

A new group of people will be entering into your life this month, however, considering that Saturn is moving through your room of friends and other people, you may be a little hesitant about allowing these folks into your life. Well, you can either choose to let these people in, clear your karma and learn from your past mistakes, or you can continue on by yourself, never clearing your karma, never growing, and never seeing the higher side of yourself. The choice, as always, is totally up to you. However, if you do decide to let these people in, there are some really good financial opportunities connected to them. Universal energies are bringing to you some really good opportunities. What you do with them is totally up to you.

Uranus has moved back into your room of health and the physical body. Is there something here that needs to be taken care of? Of course there is. Uranus is moving retrograde in the sign of Aquarius, the sign that rules speech, communication, expression and the talent. There is something your body needs to express. The Dragon's Tail is at this time moving through your room of communication, in the sign of Scorpio, also assisting you in releasing what needs to be expressed and communicated. You have many ideas, talents and skills that are locked away inside of your body. The Dragon's Tail and retrograde Uranus are both working together to unlock these and bring them forth. Do your best to work with these planetary energies so that your gold may be exposed to you.

(September 2003)

LIBRA
SEP. 23 - OCT. 22

This is your month of preparation for your next birthday. Not only will your physical age be celebrated, so will your spirituality.

Libra, your place within this world is about to present itself to you.

Pluto transiting your third room of communication is bringing forth many talents of your soul. Within your souls being is a very perfect way of communicating and expressing yourself to the world, your talent. This talent could be writing, singing, acting, poetry, painting, dancing, etc. The true talent of your soul is working to come forth at this time. All you need to do is pay attention to the messages you receive. Pluto will transit the sign of Sagittarius until December 2008.

The Dragon's Head continues to move through the sign of Taurus, in your room of the partner's resources. This planetary aspect is making it very possible for you to attract assistance to you. What is it you desire to do at this time? Have you recognized your talent? All you need to do is put forth the effort and someone you will come in to assist. The better you do, the better the assistance you will attract to you. Planetary energies are moving in a very positive way around you, providing you with everything you will need in order to attract to you the things you want. Venus moves into your Sun sign on the 15th and will transit here until October 9th. Venus will magnify your outer appearance and cause everything about you to glow. This is a fine time of attracting. Some of you will attract a new career and some of you will attract a new love. This is actually a time of attracting someone to you to listen to your idea or plan. As Pluto continues its transit through the sign of Sagittarius, in your room of communication, a very perfect plan, idea or talent will expose itself.

Mercury returns direct on the 20th in the sign of Virgo, in your room of karma and spirituality, making this a very good time to approach someone with a plan or idea you may have. Planetary activity is all in the right place for you to first present your idea, second, to attract assistance.

Mars returns direct on the 27th in your room of health, providing you with an extra boost of energy. Whatever has been ailing you is about to be healed by the power of Mars.

(September 2003)

SCORPIO
OCT. 23 - NOV. 21

Scorpio represents the spiritual. Your opposite sign Taurus represents the physical. As the Dragon's Tail sweeps through your Sun sign and the Dragon's Head moves through your room of partnership and close relationships, these planetary energies present a time of assisting and caring for others. This is a time of taking your spirituality and physically assisting others. Much of what others are going through your soul has already been through. This is a time of remembering who you are through those whom you attract to you. Many will come to you for some sort of healing. This is a time for you to figure out just how you are to heal another. You are about to attract many people to you, many whom you have not seen in a while, and many new ones. This is a time of taking your highest Scorpio self and heal the people.

Mercury returns direct on the 20th in the sign of Virgo, placing this energy in your room of social and friends. Jupiter, planet of abundance, is already moving through this area of your life. Again, you are about to attract many old and new faces to you. Why are all of these people coming around you? They desire to be healed, and you Scorpio are the sign of the spiritual healer. Many of you will have different tools to use to do this healing that is upon you.

Whatever your soul has come to do for the people, do it the best you can. Pluto transiting through the sign of Sagittarius says "Perfect Individual." Pluto is moving through your room of money and material possessions. You must allow your absolute highest to come forth with all you do, for Pluto is perfection, and in order for you to receive in the highest, you must put out the highest.

As the Dragon's Tail sweeps through the sign of Scorpio, all that has been unknown will suddenly become known. Things that have been hidden will be seen. Secrets of the past will now be known. Things that have been lost will be found. Whatever has been kept from the world will be given back to the world. Scorpio also rules karma, letting us know that many events of the past are about to repeat themselves. Why? These things need to be cleared. Apparently they were not done in the highest before. Now it is time for these things to come back around. For you Scorpio this karma has to do with many women and children. As these events of the past resurface, face them, clear them, release them and move on. The more you clear, the better you will feel.

October 2003

(October 2003)

SAGITTARIUS
NOV. 22 - DEC. 21

Planetary energies are moving towards your room of karma and spirituality. Even though there will be many people and many social events coming up around you, you may still want to spend much of your time alone. This is a good time of year for meditation and prayer. This is a time of connecting with your higher self and your spiritual guides to receive a vision of what you will be doing in the upcoming year. I know it is only October, however, the New Year will be here before you know it. Who wants to wait until the last minute?

Planetary energies are bringing around a few friends whom you have not seen in a while. I know there is other things you may rather be doing at this time, however, do your best to connect with your friends and your past at this time. Planetary energies are moving through your room of karma.

Jupiter continues to transit through your room of Career. What a wonderful place for this energy to be. Jupiter is enhancing your place within this world. Your masculinity is coming forth and your ability to lead is magnificent. However, don't let this power take over you. This is extreme power you are dealing with and one can easily get carried away. I am sure you are happy with your present position, however, just remember to stay in your highest and don't let arrogance become a part of your character. This is a wonderful time for many of you, and I am very happy to see you where you are.

Saturn will go retrograde on the 25th of this month in your room of Sex, Debts and the Partner's Resources. Saturn is the lord of karma, bringing back events of the past to be taken to higher ground. Saturn in this area of your life has brought forth many old karmic debts. There are a lot of people whom your soul owes many "favors." Give back to those who once gave to you. And if these people are not around, make sure you assist others who need your assistance. The reason you have gotten to where you are this day has a lot to do with someone helping you out. Now it is you turn to help out another.

Mars is moving through your home, bringing forth an incredible energy to change a few things around. During your free time this month, go through your home and make a few changes. There are things there that are ready to be thrown out. Make room for the new.

(October 2003)

CAPRICORN
DEC. 22 - JAN. 20

Neptune returns direct this month in your room of money and material possessions. There is either new work coming in or a change in what you have been doing. Neptune moving through this area can make it very difficult for one to attain money, that is, if you just don't know how to use this power in its highest. Neptune is the energy we use to take us beyond the physical. Right now, Neptune is transiting through the sign of Aquarius, the sign of communication and expression. Neptune in Aquarius says communication in its highest. What is your gift or talent of communicating in the highest? What is it you do? This is a time of taking whatever it is you do to a new level, moving beyond the physical. The Universe wants to greatly bless you through this incredible vibration of Neptune; however, one must learn how to use its energy in the absolute highest in order to receive in the highest. Just remember, Neptune in Aquarius says take whatever you are doing upon the Earth and take it a new level. This is a time of advancing your skill.

Saturn (lord of karma) will move into retrograde position on the 25th of this month. Saturn is moving through your room of partnership and close relationships. Saturn moving through this area of your life has brought forth many karmic duties and responsibilities. As Saturn goes retrograde, its energy will be relaxed for the next 4 1/2 months, presenting to you a time to take a break from your karmic duties with others. This is a very good time for you to connect more closely with those whom you have had many difficulties with. Use this time to make amends and peace, for when Saturn returns direct, the karmic energy will begin to flow again. Just do your best not to create more bad karma.

As Jupiter moves through your area of Higher Knowledge, Education and Travel, this is a very good time to get away, if you haven't already. Jupiter is the planet of abundance. Jupiter is creating an incredible opening for you to attract many trips to you and much knowledge. This may even be a time of study for you. Looking around your chart, this looks more to be a time of getting away from the same old, same old and allowing new things and new people to come into your life. A female friend you have not seen in while returns this month. This is someone who may need your assistance for a while. Saturn will be moving retrograde this month, this is your time to relax.

(October 2003)

AQUARIUS
JAN. 21 - FEB. 18

Planetary energies are looking very good for you Aquarius. This months New Moon will line up with Mercury, Venus and the Dragon's Tail all in the sign of Scorpio, in your room of career. Scorpio is the sign that rules karma, situations and things from the past. The job situations you attract to you within this lifetime are things you have done in previous lifetimes, and are here to return to those situations and take them to the next higher level. In other words, plain and simple, you have done these jobs before in previous lifetimes. You will attract the same work situations to you as before (previous lifetime) only so you can take what you are doing to next level. Planetary energies are supporting you. This month, you will either attract a new job situation (which isn't new to the soul) or an advancement of some sort with what you are already doing. All you need to know to make your work situation work in the highest for you is that your work situation is something your soul has returned to make better. No matter what work situation you are in, do your absolute best with it. Also realize that those whom you attract to you (other people) through career are karmic relationships from lifetimes ago. You will also need to clear these energies and take them up to a higher level. Right now, as Pluto moves through the sign of Sagittarius, each of us is going through a perfection of the individuality. We are realizing who we are and where we stand within this world. Some of us are meant to be leaders, and some of us are meant to be followers. Which are you?

Mars is moving full-force in your room of money and material possessions. This is a time for you to attract a nice little raise, or perhaps this is new money coming in from a new career. Either way, Mars is blessing you with the power of attraction as it moves through this area of your life. Hold out your hands, it is time for you to receive.

The Dragon's Head continues to take you through the lessons of the mother. This is a time of clearing old issues with a parent. Many of you will go through the loss of a parent or nurturing one in your life, due the sweeping of the Dragon's Tail in your room of the father. Yet, the main lesson that is being taught here through the activity of the Dragon is parenting. Perhaps this is a time of doing for your parent as they have done for you. There is a great reward that awaits if you do your job in its highest.

(October 2003)

PISCES
FEB. 19 - MAR. 19

Your mind and body are about to burst and overflow with many exciting ideas coming in from your soul. Grab the nearest piece of paper and begin to write. You will find your daydreaming often, for the higher mind is reaching out to converse with you. There are many messages your soul wants to tell you. All you have to do is be quiet and listen.

You will want to continue using extreme caution when driving or operating heavy machinery. This planetary energy is taking place in your room of travel, indicating that as you are driving, you will find yourself in heavy daydreams, wondering how you got from one place to the other. Avoid as much driving as possible. Ask someone else if they will drive you around. Just make sure it's not another Pisces.

This daydreaming you are about to experience is God talking to you. All you can really do at this time is be still, be quiet and listen. There will be some very powerful messages coming in at this time.

Planetary energies have worked very hard to pull you into the home. There have been many things for you to attend to there. For those of you who have children, they will be somewhat irritated at how you have been parenting them lately. (These children might be your own, someone else's, a friend or family member.) These individuals want you to do what they think you are supposed to be doing, mothering. As Pluto moves through Sagittarius in your area of career, the message here says, find your individuality, your place within this world. Even if this place is in the home. You will attract to you someone who is either a child or like a child who will want you to parent him or her. This is your karmic debt to this particular individual. Perhaps if this person is not your child of this day, maybe they were your children in a previous lifetime. Either way, your soul is indebted to this individual. Do not turn your back on this person. Clear your karma and parent this person in your absolute highest.

Jupiter continues to move gracefully through your room of partnership and close relationships, making this a fantastic time to connect with a lover. For those of you who are not in a committed relationship, you soon will be. Jupiter moving through this area of ones life brings forth commitment. Many of you will marry under this transit.

(October 2003)

ARIES
MAR. 20 - APR. 19

Planetary energies are making it very possible for you to attract a certain amount of income from the partner. The New Moon, Mercury, Venus and the Dragon's Tail will all align within the area of the partner's resources, creating an opening for additional money to come in through the partner or perhaps someone else. These planetary energies are lining up in the sign of Scorpio, which is the sign that rules karma, letting us know that something you have done in the past is about to pay off. You see, no matter what we do, we are always rewarded. The Universe never forgets.

Aries, you are the sign of the child, and every time I look at your chart, I think of the children. Planetary energies are letting us know that our children have been having somewhat of a difficult time with the mother. Our children need more old-fashioned love, nurturing and care. Saturn moving through your area of the home / mother tells us that there are issues and / or concerns pertaining to the home / mother. Do you want to move? Are there challenges taking place there that you'd rather not deal with at this time? Do not walk away nor run away from these issues. Face them, clear them and release them. Saturn's energy here tells us that these are issues that have taken place for a very long time. It's time we face these things and clear them.

Neptune returns direct this month, bringing back around someone who may have deceived you sometime ago. Neptune is moving through the sign of Aquarius in your area of friends and acquaintances. Be aware of those whom you befriend. Not all are on the up and up. You, being an Aries, will not see this right away, for you do carry the energy of the child. Check with your "mom", first.

Pluto, moving through the sign of Sagittarius, continues its transit through your room of Higher Knowledge and Travel. This area also represents the law. Many of you will attract the justice system to you for more reasons than one. This situation will have to do with a child or family member. It is up to you to find your perfect individuality within this situation. Pluto in Sagittarius within this area says you must represent the perfect truth in order to defeat this situation. Do not allow your self to lie or cheat. Stay in the perfect truth. You are being tested by the power of God (Pluto). You must represent the truth in its absolute highest or you will fail. Stand in your highest.

(October 2003)

TAURUS
APR. 20 - MAY 20

Planetary energies (The New Moon, Mercury, Venus and the Dragon's Tail) are lining up in your room of partnership, in the sign of Scorpio. Many of you will attract a love relationship to you from the past. This looks to be a very strong and powerful connection. Even for those of you who are already in a love relationship or stable marriage, someone from your past will be coming in to your life. Once in a while, planetary energies will line up in a way where an opening is created for specific things to occur. This is one of those times. It doesn't matter whether you are in a relationship or not, these planetary energies indicate a soul mate from a previous time will be coming in. The purpose of this connection is to reunite. Even here on Earth we have reunions. This is a reunion of souls. Some of you will decide to carry on with this person in a very significant way, yet others of you will just allow yourself to reunite with this soul and continue on through life. Whatever you choose to do, have fun!

Saturn will move into retrograde position in your third room of communication on the 25th of this month. Saturn has been working with you to perfect your speech, communication, the way you express yourself, or perhaps a plan / idea you've been working on. Saturn will move in retrograde position until early March 2004. This is a time of really slowing down and basically going backwards through a few things you have been working on throughout this year. Once in a while, planetary energies will go retrograde creating a lack of energy so that we may use other aspects of the self. This is just one of those times. You may feel as if your creativity level has slowed down after being so charged up for several months. Well, it has. This is a time of relaxation and taking your time. Saturn will also go backwards and pick up a few things that you have already done however have not been done in the highest, giving you a chance to go over these things once again and perfect them. Use this time of Saturn retrograde to fine-tune everything you do. Slow down and take your time.

Neptune returns direct on the 23rd of this month in the sign of Aquarius, in your room of career. Neptune's power will create wonderful visions and dreams of what you can do in the outside world, your career. Right now while Saturn is moving retrograde in your room of creativity, this is a time of planning. Use this time to write down these visions and perfect your plan. For later next year in March, your plan will have an opportunity to be manifested.

(October 2003)

GEMINI
MAY 21 - JUN. 20

Planetary energies are lining up your room of health and the physical body. Have you been a little more concerned lately about your health than usual? Well if so, good. Planetary energies within this area of your life are coming in like an x-ray. These energies are examining you from top to bottom, expanding anything that may lay hidden within the physical body, just so you may see it and know that it is there, and hopefully doing something about it. These planetary energies are moving through the sign of Scorpio (karma) bringing forth old unresolved issues that may be hidden somewhere in the physical body. The reason for this cleansing is just that. This is a spiritual examination. This is a time where the planets will expand the unresolved issues that lay hidden within you just so you can face them and clear them. This is a beautiful time of healing, especially if you realize what the physical problem really is. All illnesses within the physical body have stemmed from thought. Free your mind and use thought in the highest, and you clear your body of all disease.

Gemini, you are the sign that represents partnership and close relationships. You will always attract one who is very opposite, yet the same as you. You as an individual are very dual, which makes you a wonderful person for everyone for you are both sides of a situation. You are about to receive a message / vision about new work you will do for the land / people. You will attract your opposite so that you may heal this other side of you.

Many of you are about to take up a new profession. According to the messages in the planets, this new profession looks to be some type of care-giving work. It also looks as if many of you will take up a new study or expand on what you already know. Considering the Neptune energy moving through your room of Higher Knowledge, many of you will want to expand your conscious mind and go places you have not yet been before. Many of you will delve into metaphysical studies. Many of you will desire to visit foreign lands, and some of you will actually go. Neptune moving through your room of Higher Knowledge awakens the psyche. Planetary energies suggest that many of you are healers and this gift of healing will awaken at this time, which in turn leads one to care for another. This is a very positive time for Gemini, for your mind is about to awaken and you will see visions like never before. These visions are messages from your soul.

(October 2003)

Cancer, planetary energies are lining up in the area of home and family members. There are quite a few unresolved issues that stem from within the home. Planetary energies are lining up in this area expanding what is already there so that you may face these issues and clear them. These are past situations with your family, especially, your children or siblings. This is a time for you to face these issues one at a time and clear them once and for all. Your life wants to take you on a beautiful journey as Uranus prepares to move into your room of travel. Yet, before you can enjoy this trip in its highest, you must make room for the enjoyment to come in and be felt in its fullest. Making room means clearing your old issues. If we allow ourselves to walk around being angry with life, we cannot enjoy each moment in its fullest. So many times we look back and say, "Oh, that was such a good time." However, when we were actually walking in that moment we did not completely enjoy it for we had so many other things going on. This is a time for you to clear any thing that comes up at this time. Stop running from your past and face it. This is the only way you will be able to enjoy life right now.

Saturn will move retrograde this month in your Sun sign. Saturn first moved into the sign of Cancer in June, and will be here until mid July 2005. Saturn moving through your identity will take you back through the many lifetimes you have lived. As Saturn moves retrograde through your Sun sign, not only is its energy relaxed to the outside world, yet its energy has just gone deep within you to bring forth one of the most intense past lifetimes you have ever lived. Saturn retrograde will go deep down inside of the soul, awakening the past that you have buried the deepest. As Saturn returns direct in March of 2004, whatever this is will be revealed at that time.

Neptune returns direct on the 23rd of this month in your room of other people's money. This energy presents a time where others will be more than willing to share their resources with you. However, you will want to use extreme caution when borrowing. Neptune has a way of speaking in terms that most do not understand. In other words, make sure you thoroughly read the fine print and understand the payback terms, if there are any. If you do need to borrow money at this time, make sure it is from someone you trust. In order to attract the highest to you, you must be the highest.

(October 2003)

LEO
JUL. 23 - AUG. 22

This has been a very big year for you, Leo. Many events of previous lifetimes resurfaced. A higher truer power revealed itself through your outer being; at least this is what the planets were attempting to do with you. Neptune returns direct in your room of partnership and close relationships. Depending on who you are and how you think has all to do with the person standing directly across from you. Let's face it Leo. I know many of you have worked very hard this year to bring forth your highest self, and many of you truly succeeded, however, if you find yourself standing in front of someone whom you view as totally disgusting, please know that this person is a reflection of you somewhere in your life. This person, whoever they may be, is showing you that this energy continues to exist somewhere within you. Just face it, Leo. See whatever it is this person is presenting to you, find it within your self and take it to the next level. This is all you can do. Many of you have been in such denial for years, that your life absolutely went haywire. The last year and a half has been a little more positive for those of you who have allowed yourself to go to a higher level. The coming year promises to be even better. This month will reflect through the income you receive just how "good" of a person you have become.

Getting back to the Neptune energy that returns direct this month in your room of partnership and close relationships. You will attract to you through Neptune, either one of incredible spiritual heights, or one who is absolutely deceiving. In fact, there will be one of each. Uranus continues to move retrograde in this area also, going back within to pull forth any relationships that need to be faced, cleared and released. As you receive these direct reflections of yourself through others, once again, face them, take them to a higher level, and release them, for a higher you is preparing to present its self.

Planetary energies continue to cleanse your home. As the Dragon's Tail sweeps through this area, a deep cleansing is taking place. Venus, The New Moon and Mercury will all align within this room later this month, raising the vibration of your home, assisting you in going through everything there and hopefully releasing it. As this new you come forth, so does a new home. Our home is a direct reflection of the self. As you are cleansing your home, you are cleansing the self. A much higher vibration of your self is preparing to present itself to the world. Your new home will symbolize the new you. Congratulations!

(October 2003)

VIRGO
AUG. 23 - SEPT. 22

Planetary energies have been working with you to cleanse yourself of the past. Circumstances and situations of the past have been coming back around for the sake of being faced and taken to a higher level. Looks like many of you will write either a speech or some kind of letter to correct something you did in the past. This is a very positive step in clearing your past issues, Virgo. Take your time and think carefully about the words you will use, for remember, everything comes back around, and we want to plant good seeds only.

Saturn will move into retrograde position this month on the 25th. Saturn has been moving through your area of friends and other people since June of this year, and will remain within this area of your life until mid July 2005. Saturn has presented great lessons and challenges to you through your friends and acquaintances. Everything you have done in the past to these people is being brought back around for you to face and clear. The best way to clear these issues with others is to see yourself in them, for this is all they are doing is reflecting you right back to you.

Many of you will attract these intense reflections to you through your significant other. All that you have said and done to this person will be reflected right back at you. Yes, what this person is saying and doing is exactly what you have said and done to either this particular person or someone else. Facing these reflections of yourself is supposed to make you a better person. We will see.

Neptune returns direct this month in the sign of Aquarius in your room of health. Neptune moved retrograde from mid May of this year until the 23rd of this month. Aquarius is the sign that rules communication and expression. Planetary energies in this area of your life represent that anything that comes up in the form of illness within your physical body is related to things you have said in the past. Your diseases and illnesses have all to do with the way you have expressed yourself. If you want to clear yourself of these illnesses that lay within your body, go back through the things you have said and done. Remember the ways in which you presented yourself to others that weren't in the highest. Face these issues and clear them once and for all. Not only will these issues be cleared, yet so will the illnesses. Writing things out is also a very good way of releasing stuff, and this is a very good time of year for you to do so.

(October 2003)

LIBRA
SEP. 23 - OCT. 22

A way for you to attract additional income becomes possible this month as the New Moon, Mercury and Venus transit through your area of money and material gain. This actually looks to be something that was owed to you from the past. Or perhaps, this is an acknowledgment for a good deed you did a long time ago. Who know the reason why you should be receiving at this time? This is just destined for those of you who are walking in alignment with the will of your soul.

Saturn moves into retrograde position this month in your room of career. Saturn's energy has brought forth all kinds of stuff for you to deal with. Many of you may absolutely hate what you are doing right now, for Saturn does not make our lessons easy. You see, somewhere within the lifetime of your soul, you have done exactly what you are doing right now, in your area of career. Saturn has brought this situation back around for you to face it and hopefully take it to a higher level. Don't hate what you are doing right now. Put forth energy to do your best with it so that you can release it and create an opening for something else to come in. Considering that Saturn is in your area of career right now, you will want to face these old karmic issues, for if you decide to move on to something else, guess what, Saturn will be there also.

Libra, is there a child or family member around you who possesses a great talent? Planetary energies show there is. Neptune returns direct this month in the sign of Aquarius, in your area of children. Uranus also moves through this area, yet is retrograde at this time. Uranus actually moved outside of this area back in March into the sign of Pisces, yet went retrograde in June, bringing its energy back into your room of children. Uranus makes things happen suddenly, quickly and unexpectedly. Uranus returns direct in early November. However, until then, Neptune has returned direct. This planetary energy represents that a young one as in your child or family member around you is about to demonstrate a gift or talent of some sort. Neptune in Aquarius shows a very powerful and very high talent. Neptune's energy has been working with this individual for the last several months, assisting this person in recognizing his / her true talent. After Uranus returns direct in November, this person's talent will be more apparent. However, there is definitely something your soul is destined to do with this child. As long as you allow your soul to do what it is destined to do, you will receive greatly. Put forth your best.

(October 2003)

SCORPIO
OCT. 23 - NOV. 21

Planetary energies are lining up in a very positive way for you Scorpio. The New Moon, Mercury and Venus will all move into your Sun sign later this month.

Scorpio is the sign of karma. Scorpios have returned to the Earth to face, clear and perfect everything that lies within their soul that needs to be taken to a higher level. Scorpio is here to ascend from one level to the next. Right now, and until late December 2004, the Dragon's Tail is sweeping through your sign. Your entire being is going through a time of cleansing and perfection. Everything within your closets will go, for new things are coming in. These new things to come in will represent the new person you are becoming.

Pluto continues its transit through your second room of material wealth and receiving, letting us know that it is through your perfect individuality where you will attract to you. With all of the cleansing that is taking place within your first room of Self, a better, true you will come forth. Planetary energies are using the very best cleansing agents. By the time these energies are complete with your Sun sign, everything about you will absolutely glow. The brighter you shine the more of this material world you will receive. This is a time of putting forth your absolute best. For as you do the Universe bestows its best upon you.

Saturn will move into a retrograde position on the 25th of this month. Saturn's energy is moving through your room of Higher Knowledge and Travel. The test here is to listen. Through Saturn's energy, someone has been trying very hard to tell you something, however, because of your Scorpio sensitivity, you will find yourself not wanting to listen. Scorpio is a very psychic sign and must learn to use your gift of intuition in the absolute highest. Others will try very hard to give you their point of view, however, you being a Scorpio must use your higher wisdom. It is in the highest to listen, however, you don't have to do as someone else recommends. This is a test to you from your soul to see whether or not you will use your natural born gift of intuition. Planetary energies are working very hard to bring out the real you. The real you is a very psychically sensitive human being. First, allow your higher wisdom to come forth. Second, use it. Use this gift / talent to assist you in making the highest choices possibly. And know you need not ever compromise. Do what is always best for you.

November 2003

SAGITTARIUS
NOV. 22 - DEC. 21

Sagittarius, this is the month you prepare for the birth of a new you, your birthday, and its look to be a very nice one.

The majority of the planets will be direct this month, except for Saturn who went retrograde last month. Saturn is moving through your room of Sex, Debts and other people's money. Saturn is assisting you in attracting those old debts to you, for it is time for you to pay your bills. These may not all be monetary debts; some are just favors and assistance. Anyway, Saturn transiting through this area of your life is retrograde right now, going backwards to pick up anything it might have missed. Saturn resumes direct in early March of 2004, picking up where it left off. So, right now as you receive your income, you might want to put some aside, for when Saturn returns direct, old debts will come a knocking.

Planetary energies (Pluto, Mercury, the New Moon and Venus) are lining up heavily in your first room of Self, in your Sun sign of Sagittarius. I feel I must solute many of you for staying strong while Pluto transited your Sun sign. I know it has not been easy for Pluto is energy of perfection and has been working with you since January of 1995. Pluto's job has been to destroy the old self so that the soul may come forth and do what it has come upon the Earth to do. Pluto has been perfecting your individuality. I know there has been many times where you have felt very down and less of a person, seeming to not be able to get "it" right. ("It" being life.) Well, Pluto's transit through your Sun sign will be complete in late November 2008. So until then, make the most of it. Stop fighting with your soul and just remember to always put forth your best, for your soul is the best.

Uranus returns direct on the 8th of this month. Uranus is in its last days of transiting through the sign of Aquarius, which places its energy in your room of communication. Uranus moves on December 30, 2003. Uranus moving through your room of communication says there is a gift within this area of your life that your soul has brought with it. Could it be singing, dancing, writing, drawing, painting or what? Uranus moving through your room of communication indicates that this is a time in your life where a gift of your soul comes forth. Uranus makes things happen suddenly, quickly and unexpectedly. Whatever this talent is, it will be enhanced and taken to a brand new level through the beautiful energy of Neptune. Neptune will transit this area of your life until February of 2012.

(November 2003)

CAPRICORN
DEC. 22 - JAN. 20

Saturn continues to move retrograde in your room of partnership and close relationships. Saturn has gone deep inside of you to bring forth any and all hidden issues that need to be faced and cleared. Saturn returns direct in early March of 2004, and when it does, watch out. This will be a time for you to return to the cleansing of your karmic debts with others. And to know, Saturn has gone deep within to pull up stuff that you probably didn't even know was there. Things that have been hidden for so long I am sure you won't even recognize them as yours. Oh boy! Well, the only thing you can really do is face them and clear them. Just how bad have you been?

Jupiter continues to transit through your room of Higher Knowledge and Travel. Many of you are studying for a new job / career, for this energy of Jupiter is moving through the sign of Virgo. Some of you will travel abroad through this energy of Jupiter. However your soul is destined to use this energy, you will definitely learn a great deal of knowledge.

Mars is currently moving through the sign of Pisces, in your third room of communication and the talent. Mars will come into an exact opposition with Jupiter this month, expanding your psyche and exposing a new talent. Your mind will receive a vision of how to deal with your current situation, and this is grand. This is also something that can be used to increase your income.

Uranus returns direct on the 8th of this month, suddenly creating an open space for additional income to come into your life. Spirit says that this income will come in through a new talent that has exposed itself to you. Neptune is also passing through this area of your life, enhancing whatever this new talent is. The better you are the better you will receive. This is the message of Neptune in this area of your life. Many of you have attracted great difficulty in the area of finances. This is because your soul has been working to come forth and do what it is destined to do. Your mind (ego) has been going to a purification process as Pluto transits your twelfth room of karma. Pluto has worked hard to cleanse your mind of your own hopes, wants and desires. Pluto moving through the sign of Sagittarius says this is a time of the awakening of the soul. This is a time for you to allow your thoughts to go to a higher level. You might be able to fool man, yet you can't fool God. (God, being your higher power that lives within.)

(November 2003)

AQUARIUS
JAN. 21 - FEB. 18

Planetary energies are lining up beautifully in your room of social activities and friends. You are about to find yourself surrounded by very many beautiful people. Each one of these individuals is a reflection of you. (You knew I was going to say that, huh?) However, this is one of the most beautiful reflections I have yet seen. The New Moon, Mercury, Pluto and Venus will all line up in this area of your life, creating a wide-opened space for many wonderful social gatherings to come your way. This is a time for you to show the world that you have become. This is a time for you to share your perfect individuality with many others. I am so proud of you Aquarius.

Uranus returns direct on the 8th of this month in your Sun sign of Aquarius. Uranus has been with you since April of 1995. Uranus' job was to break down everything about you that was not in alignment with your highest self. Uranus moved through your Sun sign and got rid of just about everything that made you into the person you used to be, taking you down to the bare bones, just so your soul could come forth. Now, a totally new you is walking this Earth. Uranus will be totally complete with your outer identity December 30th.

Neptune continues to move through your Sun sign enhancing your outer appearance and making you one of the most unique persons we will ever lay eyes on. Continue to walk in alignment with this energy. It is turning you into the word magnificence.

Aquarius, you are the sign that represents communication and expression. You are the ruler of the talent. And just what is your gift to the world? You will always attract those of great knowledge to you, for you are their expression. Perhaps it is meant for your soul to enhance that of another. There is new knowledge and information upon you. It is up to you to find a way to express this knowledge and share it with the world. What are your ideas?

Mars will directly oppose Jupiter this month in a very positive place within your life, money. You have a very strong planetary opportunity to attract someone to you to promote a talent of yours. Or perhaps this is just something that is totally destined to take place. Something about you radiates throughout the world. Someone will see you and will want to take whatever it is about you to the next level. Take a deep breath and go. However, in order to attract this opportunity to you in it greatness, you must first put forth yours. Perfect your gift.

(November 2003)

PISCES
FEB. 19 - MAR. 19

It looks as if life is making better sense to you. Planetary energies show your psyche has expanded tremendously. You are receiving a better understanding of all that is taking place in your life and of all that has taken place. You may even feel as if you want to assist others in their understanding of life. Some of you will consider counseling work. Uranus returns direct in the sign of Aquarius, in your room of karma and spirituality. All of a sudden, you are going to receive a vision that will change your life totally. This newfound knowledge you receive is going to make you feel like you're going to explode. Write out what comes to you, for a time will present for you to share this knowledge on a wider scale.

Planetary energies (the New Moon, Mercury, Pluto and Venus) will all line up in the sign of Sagittarius in your room of career. You should be feeling on top of the world. Looks as if there is a lot you want to share with the world, for things are really making sense to you. Share them. The Dragon's Head continues to transit through the sign of Taurus in your third room of communication and expression, providing an opening for you to express your knowledge. I am very happy for you Pisces, for it seems that this month is a very powerful one for you.

Mars will directly oppose Jupiter this month in your first room of Self and your seventh room of partnership. Do I hear "I do?" Sounds like someone is preparing his / her wedding vows. Congratulations Pisces!

Pisces is the sign that represents the home, mother and nurturing one. The energy of the mother has gone through quite a bit in the last several years. You have been called upon to nurture everyone in your world. Yet when you needed nurturing there was no one around. That's because the true energy of the mother is pure strength. The mother energy never gets sick for she knows everything there is to know. On December 30th, Uranus will move into the sign of Pisces for the next 6 1/2 years. Uranus is sudden, erratic and unpredictable. Uranus is about to take you through a sudden, unpredictable and very intense cleansing. Uranus will break down the old structure of the Pisces energy, so that a higher vibration of the mother may come forth. Our children of this day are not necessarily wanting the old fashioned mother, yet they do not want a mom who works outside of the home all of the time either. Uranus moving through the sign of Pisces will assist us in finding that balance. You will represent to the rest of the world how it is done.

ARIES
MAR. 20 - APR. 19

You also will receive a greater knowledge and understanding of the self as the New Moon, Pluto, Mercury and Venus all line up in your room of higher knowledge. The Dragon's Tail has longed moved out of this area of your life, which made it very difficult for you to listen to others. Your mind and thoughts are clearer and things are really beginning to make sense. You may even decide to take up a new study of some sort, for your mind is exploding with ideas. Many of you will consider a new career, for something will surely attract your interest at this time.

Planetary energies have somewhat relaxed on the home front for Saturn moves in retrograde here. Saturn has been moving through this area of your life since early June of this year. Saturn came into your home tearing everything apart, bringing forth memories of the past and absolutely causing you to face a few things you may have not wanted to face. Well, now Saturn moves in retrograde, allowing things to be a little more relaxed than before. Yet, when a planet moves in retrograde, it goes deep within the soul to connect with those things that are deeply hidden. These issues will have to do with the mother and your home life when growing up. When Saturn returns direct it will bring forth all that has been hidden for the sake of these things being faced and cleared. Saturn returns direct in early March of 2004. Use this time of Saturn retrograde to clear as many of your issues as you possibly can, for when Saturn returns direct the energy will force you to do so.

Jupiter moving through your room of health at this time is blessing you with lots of energy and motivation to work. A new plan / idea reveals itself to you this month through the abundance of planetary energies lining up in your room of higher knowledge. Jupiter transiting your room of health and the physical body is intensely motivating you to carryout and manifest this idea. As long as you continue to do your work in the absolute highest, you financial situation will do wonderfully. There is a great deal of wealth that is destined to come your way through manifesting the plan of your soul. This plan will acknowledge itself to you this month. All you'll need to do is calm down and pay attention. However, how can one calm down and pay attention with Mars moving around in their head? That's right; Mars is moving directly above your Sun, causing your mind to race with many thoughts and ideas. Take a moment and write down these thoughts. This is a great way of channeling and releasing this energy.

(November 2003)

TAURUS
APR. 20 - MAY 20

Planetary activity (the New Moon, Mercury, Pluto and Venus) is lining up in your room of Sex, Debts and other people's money, creating an opening for you to receive financial assistance from another. Is there an idea or plan you have been working on that may need financial assistance? Well if so, this is a very good time for you to attract the assistance you will need. However, you will first need to perfect your plan in the absolute highest.

Taurus, you are the sign that represents the builder of the Earth. You are born with many great ideas. Your soul has come amongst the Earth to assist in its process of evolution. You are here to continually build new things for the people of the Earth. Knowing that your soul is born with many great ideas, is there something you want to do? Is there something your want to build? Perhaps you are already doing it, however, if you had difficulty finding someone to assist you with this project, it is because your plan has not been perfect. Planetary energies are supporting you in <u>perfecting</u> your plan. As soon as your plan matches the plan of your soul, the money in which you will need to manifest this plan will come in right away. This is an absolutely incredible time for you to attract the assistance you need. Let's just hope your plan is in alignment with the plan of your soul.

Uranus returns direct on the 8th of this month in the sign of Aquarius, in your room of career. Uranus is about to make something happen quickly, suddenly and unexpectedly, and it all looks very good. Remember earlier we were discussing perfecting your plan? Well, here I want to say this again. Whatever it is you are working on, perfect it in the absolute highest. There is someone nearby who will financially support your idea.

Mars will directly oppose Jupiter this month in a very positive way. Mars is transiting through your room of friends and other people. Jupiter is transiting through your room of family members. This is a very positive time of attracting others to assist you in something you want to do. The Dragon's Head continues to move through your Sun making you the one everyone looks up to. You are in a position of leadership. Many people are looking at you to see what you will do next. You have demonstrated a power of leadership and you must now follow through. Allow whatever plan your soul has brought to you to be as perfect as it can be. If the assistance just does not come through for you at this time, then it is back to the drawing board.

(November 2003)

GEMINI
MAY 21 - JUN. 20

Planetary energies (the New Moon, Mercury, Pluto and Venus) are lining up in your room of Partnership and Close Relationships. Gemini, you are about to fall in love with a perfect person. Many of you are about to attract someone new who speaks very well and very different from you. This may even be someone from another country who speaks with an accent. However, this person is extremely attractive (could be the one you are already with) and is very charming. An incredible opening has occurred in this area of your life allowing someone very unique to come into your life. Then again, this person could also be the one you are already with, and this could be the energy you will pull from him / her. Either way, this is a great time of year for love relationships.

The Dragon's Tail continues its transit through the sign of Scorpio, sweeping through the karma of us all. Whatever has laid hidden within your physical being that needs to come up and out most definitely will through the sweeping of the Dragon's Tail in your room of health and the physical body. Old memories and experiences that are unresolved will come up to the surface for the sake of being cleared. If you need assistance releasing these things from your mind, by all means go and get it. The way the planets are lining up in your room of partnership, you are destined to attract someone to you who will assist.

Many of you attracted a new home and career earlier this year. And, many of you went through a switching of places. Planetary energies have lined up in a very positive way, creating an opening for you to attract some very wonderful things to you. Remember to give thanks for all that has come your way, even though I know that much of what you have you attracted it to you. Well, remember to give thanks to yourself for listening to your soul.

This is a time of really improving your health and overall strength. Are you considering a better diet or perhaps a new line of vitamin supplements? Have you been thinking about joining a gym or maybe doing some mild exercise? Planetary energies are very supportive at this time as far as things you can do to strengthen the physical body. Allow yourself to move with the flow of spiritual activity and give your body the proper rest, nutrition and exercise it desires. All in all, this is a very positive month for you.

(November 2003)

CANCER
JUN. 21 - JUL. 22

Planetary energies (the New Moon, Mercury, Pluto and Venus) are lining up in your room of Health and the Physical body. Even though this is the month of November, your body wants to be exercised. If you are feeling the desire to eat better and take better care of yourself, know these are messages you are receiving from your soul. Perhaps there is a higher reason (and there always is) why planetary energies are motivating you to get healthy and strong. Whatever the cause may be, just do it. Take a look at yourself and allow your mind to envision how you desire to be. Once you receive the higher vision, put it into action.

Saturn continues to move retrograde through your Sun sign, going deep within your soul to dig out another one of your past lifetimes. Don't worry. Everything looks absolutely fine. Be happy that you have the chance to reconnect with the many lives you have lived. Some may not be so happy to remember, however, when these particular lifetimes awaken, take it to a new level. This is the entire purpose of rekindling with the past.

Jupiter continues to transit through your room of communication and expression. Many of you realized a new talent this year and have begun to put this into action. Jupiter is the planet of abundance and expansion and creates a wealth of overflow with all it touches. Mars will directly oppose Jupiter this month intensifying this incredible flow of energy. There will times where you will feel as if you just cannot stop talking. Perhaps you have a job using your voice; this is very good. However, much of what is running through your head at this time will need to be written down for these are many messages you are receiving from your soul and the Universe.

Planetary energies asks that you please strengthen the body at this time for there is quite a bit of traveling and out-of-the-home activity to take place very soon. Not only are the holidays coming around, there look to be something else. Prepare by strengthening the physical body.

Uranus moves into direct position early this month in your room of the partner's resources. All of a sudden, the partner comes into some additional money and will gratefully share with you. For those of you who are not in a partnership at this time you'd better go find one, for there are some wonderful things about to take place for Cancer and love relationships. Prepare by strengthening the body.

(November 2003)

LEO
JUL. 23 - AUG. 22

Leo, this has really been a happy year for you, even when planetary energies made you clean out your mother / home closets. Well, the year is coming to its end and you have survived once again.

Uranus goes direct on the 8th of this month in the sign of Aquarius, in your seventh room of Partnership and Close Relationships. Many of you will find yourself connecting with one who is physically a lot younger than you yet spiritually mature. Are you feeling like the "father" type these days? Are you feeling a need or desire to take care of someone? Planetary energies are representing a strong masculine energy moving through you at this time. It looks as if you are re-identifying with a strong masculine past lifetime. Perhaps this person whom you are about to attract to you was once your child and now the two souls are aligning to clear up old karma. Perhaps this person is still your child this day and you have recognized that there is work for the two of you to do with one another, as in business / career. This sequence of planetary energies could mean a number of things, yet one thing I know for sure is you will connect with a past lifetime soul mate who is quite a bit younger in physical age than you. Could this be the forming of a love relationship? Could be. Uranus going direct in your seventh room of Partnership will create an opening for this person to come in, and for you to recognize that there is work to be done between the two of you.

And just what is the significance of these two souls coming together? The significance is to clear old karma and to take the relationship to a new level. Some of you are already in a love relationship. This does not mean that you are to leave the one you are with and run off with this younger person. For others of you this is not that type of relationship. This could be a parent / child business relationship. Walk through this situation in the absolute highest of truth. There is absolutely no reason for any of us to continue to create bad karma, especially since we all know so much about life.

Jupiter continues to move through your room of money and material possessions, creating an incredibly huge opening for wealth and prosperity to come to you. Jupiter is moving through the sign of Virgo, which represents our career and standing within the world. Placed in your room of career is the Dragon's Head in the sign of Taurus. There is plenty of work and great success all around you.

(November 2003)

VIRGO
AUG. 23 - SEPT. 22

Planetary energies are lining up in your area of the home, in the sign of Sagittarius. Sagittarius is the sign that represents the individuality. The message I receive for you is get yourself together. Planetary energies lining up in your area of the home says this is a time to rebuild and redecorate your foundation. Our home is symbolic of the self. Take a look around your living quarters at everything that exists there. Does everything that exists within your home represent you? If not, get rid of it. Planetary energies lining up in the sign of Sagittarius says that this is a time of perfecting your individuality, uniqueness and oneness. This is a time of re-finding yourself.

Mars will directly oppose Jupiter this month. Jupiter is transiting through your first room of Self as Mars moves through your seventh room of Partnership. Mars challenges every planetary energy that exists. It is such a competitive planet. Jupiter is usually very happy and abundant, multiplying everything it touches. Mars wants to be better than Jupiter. Mars wants to be better than everybody. You will attract to you a very competitive situation between yourself and another. This situation looks to be taking place within your home. Stand your ground and stay in your absolute highest. Well, if you're wrong, you're wrong, and you will need to step down and admit it. Mars opposing you is like a child. Perhaps it is important for you to be the adult. You are Virgo, and in the original astrology, you are the sign that represents the Career and Father. I suppose it's time you are who you are.

As the Dragon's Tail sweeps through the sign of Scorpio, you will find yourself repeating an incident from the past. Things surely have a way of coming back around and quickly. The Dragon's Tail is sweeping through your room of communication. It is not meant for you to yell and scream in order to get your point across, for the Tail of the Dragon does sweep here. It is meant for you to be quiet and listen. No one says you have to agree with what is being said to you. Just be quiet and listen. Realize that this situation you are in this day is a repeat of the past. Sit back and figure out a way to take this situation to a higher level. The last thing you will want to do is keep your thoughts and feelings locked inside. Write out how you feel, and perhaps allow only you to read this. After you write out your feelings, throw them away and feel the joy of peace that will overcome you. Believe me, I have done this many of times and it works.

(November 2003)

LIBRA
SEP. 23 - OCT. 22

As the Dragon's Tail sweeps through the sign of Scorpio, situations of our past will come back around. For you this energy of karma is taking place in your career and home.

Whatever you are doing in the area of career, it looks to be un-enjoyable. Not only that, this is something you have gone through before. Why do you keep allowing yourself to attract to you the same old situation? Take what you have and do your absolute best with it. Do not allow yourself to walk away from this situation as you have done in the past. See this one through to its highest completion, so that this situation never needs to repeat itself. Planetary energies are lining up heavily in the sign of Sagittarius, in your room of communication. Be like "eminem" and just say it. He's a Libra, too.

Uranus moves into direct position this month in your room of children. Is there something your soul has promised to do for one of your family members? If so, whatever it is will resurface at this time. Complete your karma with your family members so that your life may move on in a positive way. Uranus returning direct in this area of your life makes things happen suddenly, quickly and unexpectedly, like pregnancy. If this is in alignment for you to impregnate at this time, then so be it. If this is something you would rather not do at this time, then of course, you know what to do, refrain from sex. But then again, I am speaking to Libra. Anyway, it is my job to let you know what the messages are within the planets. What you do with this information is totally up to you.

The Dragon's Head moves through your room of giving. This is a time for you to learn how to give in the highest. What is giving in the highest? Let's say that something happened to one of your friends and he / she could not care for himself / herself. Your soul is destined to assist this person in care. This is the only reason you would attract something like this to you. So do you use your money to hire a caretaker for this person? Perhaps, if you have the money and can afford it. Yet, what if you don't have the money to provide a caretaker for this person? What would you do then? This is your lesson as the Dragon's Head moves through the sign of Taurus in your eighth room of Debts. Figure out a way to best assist another.

(November 2003)

SCORPIO
OCT. 23 - NOV. 21

Considering you have put forth your best, you are about to receive your best. Planetary energies are lining up heavily in your room of material receiving. The New Moon, Mercury, Pluto and Venus are all moving towards your second room of money and material receiving in the sign of Sagittarius. Sagittarius is the sign of oneness, independence and individuality. Are you independent? Can you do whatever needs to be done on your own or do you "need" someone to help you out? Can you make it on your own? Have you figured out your individual talent? Scorpio, you are going through the test of the individuality and if you pass, there is a great reward to be received.

Uranus moves into direct position early this month is your area of the home. Expect a sudden and quick change to place within your home before the year is out. Considering that the Dragon's Tail is sweeping through the sign of Scorpio, this could be a karmic event, meaning something that took place once before.

Why do we have to deal with karma? Karma is Gods way of giving us chance after chance after chance to get something right. The Universe never stops giving chances. We have from now throughout eternity to get whatever right. This is why we have karma. Scorpio, your life is all about karma. Absolutely nothing you attract to you is new. You have been around time after time, again and again. Being a Scorpio says you are on your way to a whole new level, that is, if you get it right this time around.

For those of you who are walking in your absolute highest, you are about to receive in the highest. Planetary energies represent a new home to come into your life. This home is totally symbolic of you. If you don't like the home you are about to attract to you, then by all means, change you. The better you are, the better you will receive.

As the Dragon's Head moves through the sign of Taurus, you are becoming a great healer. As the Dragon's Tail sweeps through your Sun sign, everything about you is about to change. You are going through a complete personality makeover. Death to the scorpion and life to the Eagle. Spread your wings and fly as high as you can.

Saturn transiting through your room of higher knowledge has gone deep within the soul to pull up and out the most incredible knowledge ever. Prepare to soar.

December 2003

(December 2003)

SAGITTARIUS
NOV. 22 - DEC. 21

We have come to the final month of this year, and once again, we made it through. I know it's your birthday and Christmas is upon us, however this month looks to be a very good time for receiving for you. Planetary energies are on your side. Looks like you you're going to receive lots of books or reading material. Ooops! I didn't mean to give it away. Anyway, this year has been about many things, yet mainly facing and clearing the past. You're not the only one who had to go through months of karma; the whole world went through it. Even though there were times where we felt very alone.

Mercury (our planet of communication) moves retrograde on the 17th of this month in your Sun sign of Sagittarius. We will end this year in silence, peace and recollection. Mercury has moved deep within, communicating with the soul, finding out what we are to do next. Planetary energies (Uranus, Neptune and Venus) are moving heavily through your room of communication and expression, expanding the true gift of your soul. Have you figured out just what that is? Let's hope you will this month.

Sagittarius, you are the sign that represents oneness, leadership, independence and the individuality. I know it has not been easy dealing with Pluto moving through your Sun sign, however, you must learn to stand on your own two feet. This is what your sign is all about. This has been a pretty strong year of independence; let's hope this will last.

Jupiter, planet of abundance and multitude continues to transit through your area of career. Looks like you have finally discovered who you are and what you are to do within this world. Many of you are blessed with strong communication skills. I hope you will use them more. Your creativity is strong, remarkable and beautiful. See yourself for who you really are. And once and for all, please remove that mask.

The Dragon's Tail continues to move through the sign of Scorpio until late December of 2004, sweeping through your room of karma and spirituality. Let's hope you allow yourself to do a little growing up this coming year, for you know why? Uranus will be moving into your room of the home / mother on the 30th of this month and will continue to transit here until November 2008. Many of you will become parents during this Uranus transit, and believe me; our children do not need another child raising them. Have a happy December!

(December 2003)

CAPRICORN
DEC. 22 - JAN. 20

You are preparing for your birthday as the world prepares for another year. Capricorn, you have had some pretty tough challenges to deal with this year, yet, I see you made it through. Like the old saying goes, "What doesn't kill you makes you stronger." I absolutely love this saying.

Planetary energies are making it very possible for you to have one of the best holiday seasons ever. Mars will enter into the sign of Aries and dance through your home. Expect lots and lots of playful energy to take place there.

The Dragon's Head continues to move through the sign of Taurus until late December 2004. Many of us are going through a time of caring for another. For you, this energy is moving through your room of children / family members. Planetary energies have already suggested that there was someone around whom you may have had to care for. Well, this time is not quite complete. Saturn continues to move retrograde through your room of partnership. Saturn returns direct early March 2004. Saturn transiting the seventh room of partnership has to be the most difficult transit there is for Saturn. Saturn will actually bring forth all that you have put out in the past and return it to you through another. Saturn will also bring forth past lifetime karma through this lifetime. Let's hope you have put out only good towards others, for if you have not, Saturn will let you know. Saturn's transit will be complete in this area of your life in July 2005. Until then, do the best you can possibly do with those closest to you, for you will attract intense challenging reflections.

Venus, Neptune and Uranus are moving through the sign of Aquarius in your room of money and material gain. Aquarius is the sign that rules speech, communication and the talent. These planetary energies are all working together to assist you in recognizing a true talent of your soul. In recognizing this talent, you have an opportunity to manifest this upon the Earth and in turn receive an incredible amount of wealth for allowing your soul to express its gift. Many of you will be quite anxious to recognize this talent, and I don't blame you. Not only will this bring forth monetary fulfillment, it will also bring forth contentment, and this is what we all seek.

Enjoy your holidays, Capricorn, and I hope to see you next year.

(December 2003)

AQUARIUS
JAN. 21 - FEB. 18

Happy Holidays Aquarius! Venus, Neptune and Uranus will all line up in your Sun sign this month, intensifying your outer appearance greatly. Are you preparing for some type of presentation? It sure looks like it. Mars enters into the sign of Aries on the 16th of this month, placing this incredible energy in your room of the talent. Whatever it is you are doing at this time will absolutely magnify. Your entire presence is bubbling over and many people will want to talk with you. Why are you glowing, everyone will want to know. Perhaps it is time you share your secret.

The Dragon's Tail continues to sweep through the sign of Scorpio placing this energy in your room of career. The energy of the Dragon continues to pull you into the home so that you may focus on your project. If you have been wondering why your social life has somewhat slowed down, it is because your soul wants to be in the home, perfecting its gift to the world.

Jupiter continues to transit through your room of the partner's resources creating an opening for you to attract monetary assistance. For those of you who are married, Jupiter will bring forth these resources through your partner, and what a wonderful partner you have. For those of you who are not in a relationship at this time, you soon will be, that is if your relationship door is open. Anyway, if you are in need of monetary assistance, it will be easy for you to attain with Jupiter moving through this area of your life.

This has been a year for Aquarians to come out of their closets and allow the real self to be exposed. There are many wonderful talents that exist within you; however, there is one in particular that desire to be carried out. If you are not aware of what this is, you might want to learn how to connect with your guides and receive messages from your soul, or seek out a psychic reader for assistance.

All in all Aquarius, life looks to have been pretty good for those of you who are walking in alignment with your higher self. Next year brings about even more positive things for you, if only you allow them to come in. Continue to create space in your life for spirit to work with you. And again, if you are in need of monetary support or assistance, planetary energies are making it available to you. There is a plan your soul wishes to manifest amongst the Earth. Connect with your soul and allow your mind to see what this is. Happy Holidays!

(December 2003)

PISCES
FEB. 19 - MAR. 19

Looks like everyone may be coming to your home for the holidays, and with their children. Mars moves into the sign of Aries this month, placing its energy in your second room of material receiving. Because of how wonderful you have been to others, the Universe is about to bless you abundantly. Mars moving through the sign of Aries is pure energy and this is exactly what you are about to attract. You have really made quite the impression on someone.

Jupiter (planet of abundance) continues to move through your room of partnerships. Many of you will marry under this transit, and many of you will have many dates. Jupiter's energy in the room of partnership and close relationships brings forth strong commitments and solid unions. Congratulations to those of you who are walking in alignment with this energy.

Uranus will be moving into your Sun sign December 30th until March 2011. Uranus walks through certain areas of our lives and takes us through a sudden, quick and unexpected change. Uranus job in our life is to break down our falsely built structure, giving us a chance to rebuild on a better foundation. Uranus is preparing to move through you for the next 7 1/2 years, breaking down all that is not really you so that the real you may step forth and walk this journey. Life is all about love, happiness, peace, prosperity and fun, and if we are having anything less than this, the Gods will come in and tear it all out. This is Uranus' job.

Pisces you have come a long way. You are the sign that represents the mother and the home. Your purpose within this lifetime is to nurture the Earth and the people of it. Planetary energies will continue to pull your spirit into the home for there is quite a bit of work your soul desires to do. Many of you will begin to write under this transit, for a whole new world is about to open up around you.

So, just how does one walk in alignment with his soul? We walk in alignment with our soul by moving with our inner feeling. And how does one connect with his inner feeling? One connects with his inner feelings by first getting to know it. Next, we practice by using it all the time. An incredible gift / talent that your soul has come to the Earth with is about to expose itself to you through your inner feelings. Get to know this feeling and allow yourself to use it everyday. Happy Holidays.

(December 2003)

ARIES
MAR. 20 - APR. 19

The upcoming year will take you on many journeys. Your soul is very excited and preparing for travel.

Planetary energies show a very big change is on its way. The world is about to open wide, just for you. If you have allowed yourself to walk in alignment with your soul, there is something very wonderful you have put together and you are preparing to take whatever this is all around the world. Planetary energies will greatly pull you out of the home for career looks to be most important at this time.

Mars moves into your Sun sign on the 16th of this month. Mars absolutely loves being in your sign, for it gets to play and have lots of fun without being restricted. Aries is the sign of the child; there are no rules or restrictions. However, there are laws of the land that must be followed. So when this burst of Martian energy begins to move through you, make sure you are in control of this energy and the energy is not in control of you. Mars is about to empower you for the month and a half, fueling you with great strength, energy and motivation. I know Christmas is happening this month, however this energy has absolutely nothing to do with that. I am sure you want to enjoy the holidays, however I see your spirit very excited about something else and dancing in the streets, for this feeling has all to do with your career.

As Pluto has moved through the sign of Sagittarius in your room of Higher Knowledge, the Universe has brought to you a perfect one to assist you in reaching your higher self, a great teacher. I hope you have allowed yourself to listen and trust. For when Pluto moves into your room of career, you will then present your perfect individuality to the world. You are becoming a perfect one through the one who teaches you.

Venus, Neptune and Uranus are moving through your room of other people, social and friends. This planetary alignment is bringing many creative people into your life, for this lineup in taking place in the sign of Aquarius. No wonder you're excited. You are about to connect with many people of many talents. They are coming into your life to show you the many things you are capable of doing. You are about to expand your creativity and talent through these many beautiful Aquarian people you are about to connect with. I can see how excited you are about this discovery of your new talent. Happy Holidays!

(December 2003)

TAURUS
APR. 20 - MAY 20

This is an exciting time of year for you also, Taurus. Planetary energies are lining up in your outside world, attracting many wonderful career opportunities to you.

The New Moon on the 23rd of this month will take place in the sign of Capricorn, in your room of Higher Knowledge. You are about to receive news from someone who looks to be very interested in something you do, a promoter of some kind.

Saturn has been moving through your room of communication since June, igniting an idea that has lain inside of you for quite some time. Saturn's job in this area of your life is to assist you in facing a talent or skill that lies within you. Saturn has also been trying very hard to assist you in perfecting this plan. Saturn has a very unique way of helping out. Saturn will come in, look at whatever it is you are working on and completely tear it apart. Saturn will tell you, "You can't do that; it will never work." "Do you really think someone will buy you idea? It's horrible!" Saturn will bring forth any doubt you may have pertaining to your plan. Saturn's energy will absolutely tear it apart, or totally perfect it. Realize that all Saturn is doing is magnifying your own doubts and fears. For Saturn knows that once we remove the doubt, we remove the fear, and there lies perfection. So you see, your soul has had a plan, an idea. Planetary energies have been working with you to assist you in manifesting this plan, however, there has been one delay after the other. The Universe is now making it possible for you to attract someone to you who finds your idea interesting. Work on perfecting you speech, for this will have all to do with the outcome. Do you really want to do this? Are you sure?

The Dragon's Head will continue to move through your Sun sign until late December 2004 as the Tail continues to sweep through your room of partnership. The Dragon's Tail is presenting a cleansing. Karmic relationships of the past will resurface during this sweeping for the sake of being faced and cleared. Many of you will find yourselves unable to stay connected in any love relationships at this time; this is because of the Dragon's Tail sweeping through this area. This is a time for you to clear your past so that a much better you may come forth as the Dragon's Head moves through your room of the Self. Clear your past, allow a much higher and more vibrant you to come forth and focus your energies on manifesting the plan of your soul.

(December 2003)

GEMINI
MAY 21 - JUN. 20

This year has brought about a switch in energy for you. Last year, you were the one providing for another. This year, someone has wanted to provide for you. Looks like this holiday season is bringing out your appreciation for one who has stayed by your side. The partner also looks very appreciative for what you have done for him / her. Even though planetary energies suggest that you and your significant other will come together and enjoy the holidays with your families, it also looks as if the two of you will spend much of this holiday season alone with one another.

You may feel a great need to do more giving than receiving this year, for there is something you are very grateful for. Yet, there is still quite a bit of stuff that the Universe wishes to give to you through others. All you need to do is say Thank You.

Mars moves into the sign of Aries this month, placing this energy in your room of friends, social and other people. Have you not spent much time with your friends? Well, you will this month and maybe even next. Mars is incredible energy and motivation. Your friends will be very excited to see you and be with you. Looks like you are about to do a lot of playing in the snow. Isn't great to feel like a kid again?

Uranus will move into the sign of Pisces on the 30th of this month, placing its energy in your room of career. Uranus brings forth unexpected changes. Uranus will move through this area of your life until March of 2011. Whatever it is you are doing in the outside world will go through one change after the next until the Universal energies get you where you belong. This can be a discouraging time if you don't know what's going on. However, you do know because I just told you. So you see, there is no reason for discouragement. Just know that what you attract to you from the Universe are situations to assist you in finding and connecting with your higher self. Just do the best you can do with each situation.

The energy in your home looks absolutely fantastic. Jupiter, planet of abundance, is moving through this area greatly expanding the energy here. You have really decorated your home nicely, and it looks as if you're not completely done doing all you want to do. Just take your time with this process and don't settle for less. Everything you desire to do with your home will be done exactly the way you want. Have a happy holiday.

(December 2003)

CANCER
JUN. 21 - JUL. 22

Planetary energies are lining up all around the area of partnership. Some of you will attract a love relationship and others business. Either way, both look very, very good.

Saturn has been moving through your room of the Self, bringing forth all of your doubts, fears and insecurities about you. Whatever you do not like about yourself, Saturn will come in and expand upon it. Saturn's job is to make us face our fears and get rid of them once and for all. I can see that this Saturn transformation has not been easy for you; however, it is not meant for you to get depressed and go hide away from the world. Saturn challenges you to get up and take whatever it is you don't like about yourself and make it likeable. Saturn wants you to be the best you can be, and the only way for us to be the best of who we are is to get rid of all doubts and insecurities. Saturn is moving retrograde at this time, going deep within your soul to bring forth any and all doubts and insecurities that lie deep within. Saturn will go direct March 7, 2004. You have until then to work on your insecurities without the powerful force of Saturn.

Mars moves into the sign of Aries on the 16th in your room of career. Many Cancer people do well in careers that have to do with the children. You are a very nurturing sign and always seem to put another first. As Mars moves through this area of your life, a new career may unfold, one that has to do with the children. Cancer is such a giving sign, and right now, there are many children who are seeking someone just like you to show them how to be a better person. You may not decide right away for Mercury does go into retrograde this month. However, the energy is out there. Planetary energies show that something to do with the children will present itself to you this month through your area of career.

So many of you are about to fall in love this month, for planetary energies are really connecting you with others. This is absolutely fantastic. For those of you who desire to connect with someone and fall in love, this is the time to do. A beautiful opening has been created all around your room of partnership and close relationships. All you have to do is be in the right place at the right time, and you will. Next year brings forth a lot of travel with the partner. Prepare now. Happy holidays Cancer. See you next year.

(December 2003)

LEO
JUL. 23 - AUG. 22

This has been a great year for Leos. It has been all about work, career and making lots of money. The Dragon's Head has been moving through your room of career, as Jupiter moves through your room of money and material possessions. Planetary energies have provided incredible opportunities for Leos to attract success with themselves and in the outer world. You have listened even when you did not want to and you have acted in your highest. You have allowed yourself to stay in your truth even though there were many times when it was easier to just tell a lie, but you didn't. And now, many of you have aligned with your place / standing within this world. You have figured it out and it feels good. There are still quite a few lessons your soul wishes to share with your mind. However, within the next year and a half, many of you will write inspirational stories to share with the others about your incredible journey.

Mars moves into the sign of Aries this month in your room of Higher Knowledge. Wow! You just can't stop, can you? Well, this is good. Mars is providing you with incredible energy to think. Many of us call this mental clarity. It's like all the dust and cobwebs have cleared from your head and everything is clear. Write down everything that comes to you at this time, for these are messages from your soul. These are things your soul wants to do while it is here upon the Earth. Write down these things for the mind has a way of forgetting. If you write them down now and put them away, they will manifest when the time is right. I can't state this enough. Write down these messages you receive from your Higher Self.

Even though there were times when you had to disconnect from others and others felt you were being mean, they are still by your side. Venus, Neptune and Uranus are all lining up together in the sign of Aquarius, placing this energy in your room of partnership and close relationships. The one closest to you (as in love relationship) is an extraordinary, spectacular, wonderful and beautiful person. As soon as you recognize this, you will be looking at your soul.

There is one person in particular whom your soul desires to connect with during this holiday season and that is a young male child. There is a deep soul connection between you and this person, and your soul looks as if it is ready to reconnect. Many of you may not make this connection until next month; however, I feel your soul wants you to make the necessary travel preparations now. Have a happy holiday.

(December 2003)

VIRGO
AUG. 23 - SEPT. 22

Hello again Virgo. This year has been mainly about clearing up old karma with your friends and loved ones. This has also been a year of ending old relationships and allowing new ones to form. Your words have been tested to make sure you say everything in its highest. Many have looked up to you, seeing you as the one who has all the answers, yet there have been several times where they saw you differently because of the words you used so openly. Now the Dragon's Tail sweeps through the sign of Scorpio in your room of communication, bringing back everything you have said in the past and making you face it once again. Take your time before you Speak Virgo. For everything you say will be held against you. The words you use will either make or break you.

Planetary energies are asking you to feed the children. There are different children organizations around and the Universe is asking you to reach out to one of them. You are the sign of the Father and your masculine soul wants to be recognized. Provide a helping hand to those in need.

Planetary energies are also lining up in your room of health in the sign of Aquarius. Aquarius is such a creative sign; it rules Art, color and creative expression. Within every Virgo I know lies a creative talent, whether this be painting, sewing, drawing or designing. As the Dragon's Tail sweeps through your room of the talent, one that your soul has brought in with it will come forth. This is your communication outlet. Many of you will take this talent and turn it into a moneymaking venture. And you are supported if this is what you decide to do.

Many of you may feel it necessary to spend this holiday alone with the self, for there is quite a bit your soul wishes to connect with you about. The coming New Year promises to bring forth many new people in your lives and your inner spirit wants your mind and body to be ready.

Remember to allow yourself to connect with that young person spirit spoke about earlier, for it is through this connection where you will clear much of your karma. Your spirit wishes to be the best it can possibly be, and in order to do this it needs to walk in alignment with you. Have a wonderful and safe holiday.

(December 2003)

LIBRA
SEP. 23 - OCT. 22

Your soul brought to you an event of the past that it wished to take a little higher. This has to do with a child or perhaps a family member. Planetary energies are lining up in the sign of Aquarius, in your room of the children / family members. There is something your soul set out to do for one in this area of your life. Mars will move into the sign of Aries this month bringing forth an incredible energy and motivation. An opening within the world has been created for you to find a greater success with this plan. You are the sign of many people. Libras make great promoters for they have the power to gather the people. Your soul is working very hard to come forth at this time and do what it is destined to do with this family member. Allow your soul to do what it is destined to do, and from this you will receive a great reward.

It looks like everyone will want to gather in your home for the holidays. Planetary energies have created a huge open space for many to gather there. People of all sorts and kinds are apart of your life, for each one represent the many lifetimes you have lived. See yourself and the lives you have lived through those who are closely in your life at this time. This is a great way of cleansing the soul of its karma.

Many of you will involve in a new love relationship. This is wonderful, great, fine and dandy. However, your soul does not want you to lose focus of the greater plan. This young family member comes first says the voice of Spirit. You will attract someone to you who will assist you in promoting this person to a higher ground. This is your karmic destiny. Once you do what your soul is destined to do with this person, then you are free to run around and play. Yet, you must not lose focus on the greater Divine plan. Realize whom this younger person / family member is and put forth that effort to promote.

The Dragon's Tail continues to sweep through your room of material possessions assisting you in getting rid of stuff that is no longer representation of you. A whole new life is ahead of you and much of it has to do with your promotion of this younger person. If you do exactly what is meant of you to do in its absolute highest, you will attract incredible wealth, a new home and all the mind and body can ever imagine. Yet it all has to do with how well you promote this person.

Take care Libra, and have a happy holiday.

(December 2003)

SCORPIO
OCT. 23 - NOV. 21

Mars steps into your room of health and the physical body making you feel vibrant and more alive than you have in a very long time. You will feel youthful, playful and free. Perhaps the kid in you wants to come out and play.

The Dragon's Tail continues to sweep through your Sun sign until late December 2004. The many selves you have been within your soul's lifetime are coming up and out. "Remember me?" As these many lifetimes reveal themselves, you will attract other souls who were a part of those lifetimes. Yes, there is karma for you to clear also. We all have karma to clear, especially you Scorpio. You're made of karma. You have returned to clear all of your old karmic debts so you can move on to the next level, wherever that may be. This is your lifetime to evolve.

Planetary energies have provided a new home for many of you. I hope you have used your time well and prepared your home carefully for there are others who are coming in to your home space. Uranus will move into the sign of Pisces on the 30th of this month, placing this energy into your room of children / family members. Uranus is quick, sudden and unexpected change. Have you created a space for these people to come into? Perhaps you'll want to do so now.

The New Moon will take place in your room of communication and the talent, presenting a fresh idea. Looks like this is something you can do from home and with the assistance of your family members. How nice, a family-owned business. However, Mercury (planet of communication) will move into retrograde on the 17th, so many of the decisions that will need to be made may not be decided until January. That's okay. There is no hurry.

All in all Scorpio, this has been a good year for you and for those around you. The coming new year brings forth many things for you to do with your family or perhaps those who are like family to you. Keep your energy in the highest and you will attract only the highest. Your life is all about clearing karma and taking every situation that comes upon you to the absolute highest. Stay honest in all of your dealings and do your best to see only the best in all. Confront and face your fears, for doing this will make you a greater person for the world to follow. Take care and happy holidays!

Messages of the Stars
P.O. Box 5427
Apache Junction, AZ 85278-5427
(480) 984-7447

www.messagesofthestars.com